Reflections on Translation

TOPICS IN TRANSLATION
Series Editors: Susan Bassnett, *University of Warwick, UK* and Edwin Gentzler, *University of Massachusetts/Amherst, USA*

Work in the field of Translation Studies has been expanding steadily over the last two decades, not only in linguistics and literacy studies, but also in business studies, economics, international studies, law and commerce. Translation Studies as a discipline in its own right has developed alongside the practice of teaching and training translators. The editors of the Topics in Translation series encourage research that spans the range of current work involving translators and translation, from the theoretical to the practical, from computer assisted translation to the translation of poetry, from applied translation to the history of translation.

Full details of all the books in this series and of all our other publications can be found on http://www.multilingual-matters.com, or by writing to Multilingual Matters, St Nicholas House, 31–34 High Street, Bristol BS1 2AW, UK.

TOPICS IN TRANSLATION
Series Editors: **Susan Bassnett,** *University of Warwick, UK* and Edwin Gentzler, *University of Massachusetts/Amherst, USA*

Reflections on Translation

Susan Bassnett

MULTILINGUAL MATTERS
Bristol • Buffalo • Toronto

To my brother Steve, another kind of translator

Library of Congress Cataloging in Publication Data
A catalog record for this book is available from the Library of Congress.
Bassnett, Susan.
Reflections on Translation/Susan Bassnett.
Topics in Translation: 39
Includes bibliographical references and index.
1. Translating and interpreting. I. Title.
P306.B295 2011
418'.02–dc22 2011015598

British Library Cataloguing in Publication Data
A catalogue entry for this book is available from the British Library.

ISBN-13: 978-1-84769-409-6 (hbk)
ISBN-13: 978-1-84769-408-9 (pbk)

Multilingual Matters
UK: St Nicholas House, 31–34 High Street, Bristol, BS1 2AW, UK.
USA: UTP, 2250 Military Road, Tonawanda, NY 14150, USA.
Canada: UTP, 5201 Dufferin Street, North York, Ontario, M3H 5T8, Canada.

Copyright © 2011 Susan Bassnett.

All rights reserved. No part of this work may be reproduced in any form or by any means without permission in writing from the publisher.

The policy of Multilingual Matters/Channel View Publications is to use papers that are natural, renewable and recyclable products, made from wood grown in sustainable forests. In the manufacturing process of our books, and to further support our policy, preference is given to printers that have FSC and PEFC Chain of Custody certification. The FSC and/or PEFC logos will appear on those books where full certification has been granted to the printer concerned.

Typeset by Techset Composition Ltd, Salisbury, UK.
Printed and bound in Great Britain by the MPG Books Group.

Contents

Acknowledgements vii
Introduction ix
1 Language and Identity 1
2 Original Sin. 12
3 Theory and Practice: The Old Dilemma 16
4 Dangerous Translations 20
5 How Modern Should Translations Be?. 24
6 Status Anxiety. 28
7 Under the Influence 32
8 Reference Point 36
9 Translation or Adaptation?. 40
10 Translating Style 44
11 Telling Tales 51
12 Pride and Prejudices 55
13 Turning the Page 59
14 Poetry in Motion 63
15 When Translation Goes Horribly Wrong 67
16 Living Languages 70
17 All in the Mind. 74
18 More than Words 78
19 Just What Did You Call Me?. 82

20	Lost in Translation	86
21	Good Rhyme and Reason	90
22	Women's Work	94
23	Plays for Today	98
24	Between the Lines	102
25	Playing on Words	106
26	Pleasures of Rereading	110
27	On the Case	114
28	Gained in Translation	118
29	Layers of Meaning	122
30	The Value of Comparing Translations	126
31	Where the Fun Comes In	130
32	Translators Making the News	134
33	What Exactly Did Saddam Say?	138
34	Native Strengths	144
35	What's in a Name?	148
36	Food for Thought	152
37	Family Matters	156
38	Rethinking Theory and Practice	160
39	The Power of Poetry	164
Select Bibliography		169

Acknowledgements

Without the kind permission of the editors of *The ITI Bulletin* and *The Linguist* this book could never have come into being. I am grateful to them also for sensitive, intelligent and above all helpful editing of my work over many years.

A lot of people have contributed to the making of this book in different ways and have sparked ideas that then turned into articles. I particularly want to thank Ana Raquel, Claire, Cristina, Esperança, Svetlana, Xavier and Yvonne for some unforgettable conversations that set me off along new paths. Geoffrey Moorhouse, my late beloved partner helped along the way with pithy, pertinent comments.

I especially want to thank Caroline Parker, whose skills go far beyond formatting and other secretarial expertise and who has been both an insightful critic and a good friend.

Introduction

The opening words of L.P. Hartley's novel, *The Go-Between* have become one of the most famously quoted sentences in English: 'The past is a foreign country; they do things differently there.' When I reflect on where the study of translation was in the 1970s, when I was starting to write my first book, that quotation comes to mind, for things were indeed very different back then. Not only was translation not perceived as worthy of study in a university, but attitudes to translation ranked original work as much more significant that what was considered a mere copy. Translators, poorly paid and regarded all too often as hacks with a foreign language, were not taken seriously. Never mind that millions of readers were able to read works in ancient Greek, Russian, Spanish, Arabic and countless other languages, thanks to the skill of translators; translation was a lowly activity and not something to boast about. Indeed, in the world of universities, young academics were advised not to list their translations as serious publications. Promotion prospects would not be enhanced by a list of translations, no matter how successful they may have been.

I find myself guilty of that very same prejudice when I reflect that in the opening paragraph of this introduction, I have mentioned writing my *first* book, for it was in fact the second, the first having been a translation of a book on the Renaissance city by the distinguished art historian, Giulio Carlo Argan. It was, however, the first book I ever wrote that reached a large number of readers, my first monograph in effect. Its title was very simple: *Translation Studies*.

The book came out in a series edited by the distinguished Shakespearean scholar, Terence Hawkes. His series, the New Accents, was a bold endeavour to make accessible to students around the world some of the new thinking about literary studies that had been increasing in importance in the 1970s. Titles included books on structuralism and semiotics, reception theory, media studies, feminist theory, deconstruction, postcolonialism, new historicism, just some of the many trends sweeping through the academic establishment. The series was challenging and exciting, and though it was condemned by some scholars as populist, it was nevertheless hugely successful with the readers for whom it was always intended – students.

I approached Terry Hawkes with a proposal for a book on translation, and though he was at first unconvinced, he gave me the benefit of the doubt and took me on. *Translation Studies* came out in 1980, a second edition followed a decade later in 1991, with a third edition in 2002. By 2010 the number of copies sold was higher than ever. Clearly something had happened over 30 years that has changed the level of interest in translation.

What happened were major changes that can be broadly seen as both intellectual and physical. In terms of the latter, it is undeniable that millions more people are moving around the world than was the case in the 1970s. The end of the Cold War, the changes in Chinese foreign policy meant that millions who had previously been unable to travel could now start to move more freely. Economic changes, increased globalisation, developments in mass communication have all contributed to the opening of borders, as also have other kinds of pressures – famine, years of war, political oppression and world poverty, all of which have driven people to seek new lives away from their homeland. And as people move, so they take with them their language and their cultural expectations, engaging inevitably with other languages and other cultures, in short translating for themselves and being translated in turn.

The changes intellectually reflect this increased mobility, and reflect also a rethinking of disciplinary boundaries in the academic world. Translation Studies is today regarded as a serious subject, with university programmes at undergraduate and postgraduate level, journals, academic conferences and series of books proliferating, but when I wrote my book, the term itself was barely known. I chose to title it *Translation Studies* fully aware that most readers would not understand what the title might mean because the subject barely existed. True, there were programmes for training translators in many countries, but the term 'translation studies' had only just been coined, by a small group of scholar-translators who were seeking to raise the profile of translation generally. By a happy chance, I had joined that small group following a meeting in 1975, and at what has come to be remembered as a seminal conference in Leuven in 1976, the group that comprised James Holmes, Itamar Even-Zohar, Josè Lambert, Gideon Toury, Raymond van den Broek and André Lefevere set out a kind of manifesto for what they hoped would be a new field of study. Such a field would bring together research from various disciplines and would bridge the gap between translation practice and the history and theories of translation, and in so doing the status of translation would be raised. Even-Zohar proposed that any study of the history of literature must also be a study of the history of translation, for through translation new ideas, new forms, new concepts can be introduced. He also argued that the number of translations produced at given moments varies according to the stage of development at which a culture finds itself; hence, cultures in transition tend to translate more texts as they seek to consolidate, while those that see themselves as self-sufficient tend to translate less. The present boom in translations in China is a good example of the former situation, while the paucity of translations into English reflects the global dominance of that language and the sense of superiority that unfortunately accompanies that dominance.

André Lefevere was given the task of outlining what a field known as Translation Studies might consist of, and in the subsequent publication of collected papers from the Leuven colloquium, he proposed that the name might be adopted for the discipline that concerns itself with 'the problems raise by the production and description of translations' (Lefevere, 1978). This means that within the field, both the process of how a translation comes into being and what the translator does to a text are as valid an object of study as is the fortune of a text once it passes into another language and literature. Lefevere was at pains to note that theory and practice should be indissolubly linked, and should be mutually beneficial to one another. It was with these ideas in mind that I wrote *Translation Studies* as an introduction to what we all hoped would be a new interdisciplinary field.

The growth of the subject is not only due to a small group who met in Belgium in the 1970s. There are other important centres of research into translation, some more closely connected to linguistics, others to interpreting. Today, the subject is well-established, and there is a growing body of work coming out in China, Africa and India, as well as in Europe and the Americas. As I reflect on what has happened in the field over the past 30 years since the first appearance of *Translation Studies*, and consider where the subject is today, the lack of recognition of translation back in the 1970s does indeed seem to belong to another country.

Revaluing the Translator

Academic programmes about translation lead students to examine the ways in which ideas about translation have changed over time, to study theories of equivalence and problems of interlingual transfer, to investigate ideas of untranslateability and theories of meaning, to work on huge linguistic corpora, to do research on specific case studies, investigating genre, stylistic features, patterns of lexicon and syntax. The emphasis of programmes in different places varies, and there are a wide number of approaches, some more theoretical and historical, others more practically oriented and geared to the training of translators. There has also been a greater rapprochement between the training of translators and the training of interpreters, which is timely and important.

What has been less explored, however, is the impulse that leads to translation in the first place, for apart from obvious commercial factors, it is clear that a great many distinguished writers have also chosen to translate works written by other writers, and it is clear also that translating is a profession that for some people is akin to a vocation. Yet it remains a curiously marginalised profession in some countries, most notably in the English-speaking world, where only a tiny percentage of books published annually are translations, a profession that is not well-remunerated or well-recognised, despite its obvious importance in a world that sets such a high value on instant communication.

Umberto Eco, the Italian writer is fascinated by translation, not only because he himself translates, but also because he can see what happens to his own writing when someone else translates it. He even goes so far as to say that he believes that anyone studying translation should have the experience of translating and being translated so as to fully grasp the complexity of the processes involved. He is fortunate in being able to talk to his translators and so understand what they are seeking to do with his writing, and he is also aware that translation involves much more than the linguistic. In his essay, 'Translating and being translated', Eco argues that translators must take into account rules that are broadly cultural, and gives as an example of the simple phrase 'donnez-moi un café', 'give me a coffee' and 'mi dia un caffe'. These three sentences are linguistically equivalent and all convey the same proposition, but are not culturally equivalent:

> Uttered in different countries, they produce different effects and they are used to refer to different habits. They produce different stories. (Eco, 2001: 18)

He does not go into detail about what those different stories might be, but is referring to the very different practices of coffee drinking in the three cultures. He might also have had in mind the different levels of politeness in the three sentences, for while it is acceptable in Romance languages to use an imperative, in British English a request for coffee would have to be accompanied by 'please' or it could cause offence. The point Eco is trying to make is significant: translators need to be aware of the culturally determined nuances that underpin texts. What translation does is to focus attention on difference, because the task of the translator is to negotiate difference, to find ways of avoiding homogenisation while at the same time ensuring that difference does not cause misunderstanding. It is an extremely difficult task, hence the appropriateness of a bellicose metaphor often used to describe translation, as a kind of no-man's-land. Usually we think of no-man's land as a stretch of terrain between warring armies, often heavily mined, so that anyone trying to make their way through such a space will be in greatest danger. The translator, delicately stepping through the minefield, is wary of snipers watching from both camps, wary also of becoming entangled in coils of barbed wire.

It can be argued that translators have to translate not only the words on a page but the absent context in which those words appear, the text behind the text, as it were, if they are to avoid the perils of literalism and create something worthwhile. Herein lies the great dilemma for a translator: if he or she is endeavouring to be respectful to the original, then how much scope is there for textual variations? Is it licit for a translator to change a text, to add to it or delete, or does the translator have a responsibility to the original author to try and ensure that as much as possible of that author's work is brought across into the target language?

This has been discussed countless times and throughout the ages, and is both highly relevant and completely redundant at the same time. For it is simply not possible to bring any text written in one language into another without changing it; what continues to be debated is the extent of the change. Some translators have declared their intention to be absolutely faithful to an original, while others have announced that they feel free to take the liberties necessary to produce a good result. Some translators prioritise the original author, others put their readers first. We may smile today when we read the statement by Antoine Houdar de la Motte in the preface to his translation of the *Iliad* into French in 1714, when he announces that he has followed 'those parts of the *Iliad* that seemed to me worth keeping', while changing anything he thought disagreeable, but the smile changes to astonishment when we learn that he cut out half the poem, speeded up the action, invented new material and changed the behaviour of characters in accordance with societal norms of his own age:

> I have not deprived the heroes of their unjust pride, which often appears as 'grandeur' to us, but I have deprived them of the avarice, the eagerness, and the greed with which they stoop to looting, since these faults would bring them down in our eyes. (de la Motte in Lefevere, 1992: 30)

De la Motte, however, was being true to the taste and norms of his age; in London, Shakespeare was reconstructed for audiences unwilling to cope with his barbarity (the tragic end of *King Lear*, for example was softened by the recovery of Cordelia) and Voltaire pointed out that Homer needed to be softened and embellished by his translators, because a writer always writes for his or her own time, and not for the past.

Charles Tomlinson writes that great translations are as rare and as commanding as great poems. He declares that a good translator is 'either "transfus'd" by the soul of your original or you are nowhere'. A major translator can bring about a metamorphosis, can transform a work from another time and place into a dynamic, vibrant work for his or her own time, can 'transform the energies of past civilization' (Tomlinson, 1982): This idea of metamorphosis is crucially important, for as Walter Benjamin has pointed out, the translator can do more than transform past energies, the translator can effectively bring a dead work back to life, can effect a metempsychosis, whereby the soul of an original assumes another form in another language. We may ask ourselves what kind of transformation de La Motte was effecting when he cut Homer and reshaped him for French 18th century readers. Looked at from one point of view, he was betraying Homer through reductionism. But looked at from another perspective, he was bringing his own version of Homer to his contemporaries.

What makes translation different from other writing is that there is always a reading process involved prior to the actual writing itself. A translator has to become familiar with a text, has to read and reread it, seeking to understand its intricacies, for only then can the task of translating begin. Some translators became obsessed by their work, like the aged Queen Elizabeth I, compulsively scribbling her translation of Boethius as her health and spirit failed, some return over and over again to the same writer, like Michael Longley, the Irish poet who has spoken of being 'Homer-haunted' for 50 years and who used a translation of a passage from *The Iliad* as a means of writing 'Ceasefire', his magnificent poem about the cease-fire in Northern Ireland.

The detective fiction writer, Dorothy Sayers decided in mid-life to translate Dante's *Divine Comedy*. Her biographer, Janet Hitchman describes her passion for Dante as 'her last great love affair', arguing that as much as she loved any living person, she loved Dante (Hitchman, 1975: 185). In an essay about my own translation work, in the book that Peter Bush and I co-edited, *The Translator as Writer* I also used the language of a love affair to describe the relationship I had with certain writers, especially with Luigi Pirandello in the 1980s and then with the Argentinian poet, Alejandra Pizarnik in the 1990s. The love affair between translator and original author can last a lifetime, or, as in my own case, can last a few years and then fade away, but out of the intensity of the relationship can sometimes come inspired translations. Ezra Pound, one of the greatest translators who worked in many languages, ancient and modern, was all too aware of the limitations of translation, yet strove to overcome what he saw as unsurmountable obstacles.

Pound identified three kinds of poetic components: *melopoeia* which means the musical property of words, *phanopoeia* or the casting of images on the visual imagination and *logopoeia*, 'the dance of the intellect among words'. Of these, he argues that melopoeia can occasionally be appreciated by a foreigner with a particular sensitivity to sound, but that it is practically impossible to transfer this quality from one language to another. Logopoeia cannot be translated at all, though it might be possible to find a way of paraphrasing, but phanopoeia can 'be translated almost, or wholly, intact' (Pound, 1954: 25). This view of poetry and translation reflects Pound's insistence on the importance of the image, but on balance, his assessment of what is and is not translatable is accurate. The sound patterns of one language cannot be translated, nor can complex word play, whereas imagery does have a chance of surviving the transition from one language to another. Pound was writing strictly about aspects of poetry; he would have readily acknowledged the impossibility of trying to translate culture-bound elements, which takes us back to de la Motte's decision to remove what he saw as digressions about armour and the anatomical details of wounds. De la Motte was bringing Homer into Parisian drawing rooms, whereas Homer's epic was conceived in an age where heroic deeds on the battlefield, the quality of weaponry and the ability to withstand pain determined not only the status of a warrior in this life, but his reputation after death.

The essays collected in this book are reflections on aspects of translation published over a 10-year period, mainly in *The ITI Bulletin*, the journal of the Institute of Translation and Interpreting and, in some cases, in *The Linguist*. They are written for readers with an interest in aspects of translation; those readers include professional translators and interpreters, scholars, students and anyone who cares about the movement of languages across boundaries.

The essays were never intended as a contribution to scholarship, but as a means of offering insights into diverse aspects of translation that kept catching my attention. Topics include the translation of different literary genres, in particular poetry, news and media translation, linguistic problems and aspects of cultural translation. There are essays on the translation of humour, on the language of kinship, on gestures, on jokes, even an essay on what happens when translation goes horribly wrong. Through the years of writing these essays, I have been encouraged by feedback from readers, and have greatly enjoyed developing different themes.

It has also been a challenge to write in an accessible manner for all readers, not just for those located in the university environment. Translation plays such a huge role in today's world, and the majority of those engaged in translating are not academics. At the end of this book there is a bibliography giving suggestions for further reading, so that anyone who wants to follow up some of the ideas may be helped to do so, but it is my hope that these essays will be read primarily for what they were always meant to be: as one woman's reflections on what it means to be engaged in translation.

Susan Bassnett

Chapter 1
Language and Identity

Probably the best way to begin thinking about questions of language and identity is to start with oneself, with the problematics of one's own identity. This is precisely the strategy employed by the great critic George Steiner, for example. Writing about himself and his multilingual background, Steiner tells us that he has no recollection whatever of a first language, a mother tongue that took precedence over other languages acquired in babyhood. 'So far as I am aware,' he wrote in *After Babel*, 'I possess equal currency in English, French and German' (Steiner, 1975: 120). Tests of his ability to perform differently in these three languages, have, he claims, revealed no significant variations of either speed or accuracy. He is a trilingual native speaker, in whose life English, French and German have held equal sway, with the Austrian-Yiddish, Czech and Hebrew of his family hovering somewhere close by.

Steiner's story is a common one in many parts of the world, where children grow up speaking several languages with apparently equal ease. Indeed, as the global influence of English spreads and spreads, even more people are becoming bi- or multilingual. What is interesting about Steiner's case, however, is that he uses his own experience in order to raise some fundamental issues with his readers. Does a polyglot mentality operate differently from a monolingual one he asks, do all his languages really exist on the same level, or are they somehow stratified, and if so, is one language lower down in the strata, more profoundly located in the body somehow? He raises question after question, culminating in the most profound question of all:

> In what language am I, suis-je, bin Ich,
> when I am inmost?
> What is the tone of self? (Steiner, 1975: 125)

In his attempt to engage with this fundamental question, Steiner chooses to examine the complex processes that occur in translation, when a text passes from one language into another, and I shall follow his example. But first, I want to tell the story of another person, and what kind of questions she has pondered throughout her life as a person with more than one language in her head.

This child was born to monolingual parents, but taken at an early age to another country where she quickly learned to speak a second language. She happily used both languages equally until she saw something interesting: she saw that not everybody around her could use two languages, and that she might be able to use that fact to her own advantage. She has no memory of this at all, but her mother has told her how she would pretend that she could only understand Danish with English speakers, or only English with Danes, and that she could be caught out only by someone else who had equal command of the two languages, someone who, like her could change in mid-sentence and slide between both languages, in and out like a serpent from its lair.

Time passed. The child left Denmark and moved to another country. Here the memory of the Danish began to fade, but was speedily replaced by another language, by Portuguese in fact, a totally different language altogether. The girl has strong memories of these years, and can remember conversations, stories and books that she could only have encountered in Portuguese but which are remembered in English. And then came yet another country, yet another language, and by now the child was old enough to be studying ancient and modern languages in secondary school, learning Latin or French through the medium of the fourth language she had acquired in her short life, a language in which she often dreams, even though she has lived in England for many years now.

As you may guess, this is my story, a story of a different kind of multilingualism, in which languages exist differently in my head than Steiner's do for him. For each new language acquired in childhood pushed out the previous one, with the exception of English that stayed constant in the home. Years later, studying Danish formally at university in an attempt to regain it, I spoke with an Italian accent, and every new language learned from childhood, be it French, German or Spanish has been learned with an Italian, not an English accent, because Italian was the language that acted as a bridge for me, the medium through which I began formal study of languages ancient and modern after so many years of acquiring languages from other children or from servants or by osmosis from the world around me.

Some years ago I met a dialectologist who was interested in my English pronunciation and persuaded me to allow her to record me speaking so that she and her colleagues could analyse the patterns of sound. After a few weeks she came back to me, with virtually a linguistic biography: the team had picked up the Italian, the Portuguese, traces of American English (my husband's influence), vowel sounds from the north of England (my parents) and finally, miraculously, traces of a Scandinavian language. After 20 years the Danish had not died away, it had merely been submerged somewhere, making its way slowly back to the surface in a couple of particular phonetic elements.

George Steiner asks what the tone of self is. It is a question that follows logically from his own multilingual experiences and from his personal and intellectual history. My starting point, however, is different. I have never asked myself that question, because I have always seen the various languages in my head as rather like the skins of an onion: peel them away and you have nothing left. Steiner's world view is based on geology, on strata and sedimentation. Mine is a liquid metaphor: languages flow like currents, linguistic tides have come in and gone out for me, my languages are in constant motion. At different times in my life, different languages have been important, sometimes because I spoke them, at other times because I desired to learn them, at still other times because my life led me into contact with them. But what has always been central to my thinking about languages is that languages articulate the culture in which they are used, and so any examination of language needs also to take into account the broader picture.

Let me give a trivial example: social practices vary from culture to culture, expectations vary and what is permitted varies. Think for a moment how different cultures even in Europe talk (or not) about the body. When asked how you are in English, you must not tell the asker. In Middle England the standard greeting goes even further: 'How are you? Alright?' people say, or even just 'Alright?' as though willing you to say anything different and potentially disturbing. Yet in Italy, one can talk happily about medical problems, even sharing information on symptoms and cures. And Italians seem to talk a great deal about digestive problems: livers, for example, or kidney problems. Americans talk about allergies all the time, often attributing mysterious symptoms to allergies, whereas Russians would attribute similar symptoms to changes in pressure. What this means, of course, is that one can have different kinds of conversation about different topics in different languages. I always talk about my health in Italy; I never do likewise in England. Does this mean that one undergoes a kind of personality change when one changes languages? The evidence leads to such a conclusion. For languages not only have different structures through which reality is articulated, they have different vocabularies, different traditions and different histories.

Attitudes to multilingualism also vary considerably. In previous generations, multilingualism was seen as desirable and as the proper aim of any educated person. Queen Elizabeth I spoke and wrote in several languages and was still translating classical texts in her 60s. Byron and Shelley, as educated young men of their time, travelled through Europe changing languages as they went, their confidence bolstered by firm foundations in Latin and Ancient Greek. In contemporary India, multilingualism is desirable and necessary, as it is in Hong Kong, where so many people move between Mandarin, Cantonese and English on a daily basis. But in the 20th century, in the English-speaking world especially, attitudes to multilingualism became complex and troubled, illustrating another important dimension that we must never forget: languages are rarely equal, reflecting the hegemonic position of certain cultures. Our very terminology of 'majority' and 'minority' languages reflects this. Some languages are seen as important, some not and their survival often depends on that perception of difference.

In the United States, where the all-embracing figure of the Statue of Liberty personified the melting-pot philosophy, immigrants were encouraged to shed their past and acquire English, the language of their new country, of the future, of progress and of modernity. Significantly, early research on the intellectual progress of bilingual children in US schools suggested that bilingualism was basically bad. Bilinguals performed less well in IQ tests, unsurprisingly since, as we now know, the tests were designed for monolingual speakers, the second languages was seen as interfering with intellectual advancement and in some extreme studies bilingualism was viewed almost as a learning disorder. Happily, we have moved on a long way from those early perceptions of the value or valuelessness of having more than one language, but residual traces of that attitude still remain. The battle over the desirability of Spanish as a second language in US schools, for example, is by no means completely over, and there is a powerful argument that claims that children need to learn the language that will be advantageous to them later in life rather than a language that is marginalised. In Britain, the battle over standard English is similarly one that arouses strong feelings on both sides. The Newbolt Committee report of 1921 declared that class divisions were perpetuated by the existence of different varieties of spoken English, a different state of bilingualism if you like, but bilingualism nevertheless:

> Two causes, both accidental and conventional rather than national, at present distinguish and divide one class from another in England. The first of these is a marked difference in their modes of speech. (Newbolt, 1921)

The second difference was 'undue narrowness of the ground on which we meet for the true purposes of social life' (Newbolt, 1921). The Newbolt Committee contrasted the pride of French artisans in their native language and culture with the lack of a sense of national pride in their English equivalents and expressed the wish that all classes might be united in a common love of English language and literature in the future. The road to a united society was felt to lie with linguistic consensus.

But the divisiveness that the Newbolt Committee discusses derived not from a very clear linguistic policy, one that had sought to establish a dominant form of spoken English over all other variants. This hierarchical view was also in line with a wider language policy: that of seeking to impose English over other languages in the British colonies. And just as the history of colonialism and imperialism has been dominated by attempts to impose the language of the conquerors over the conquered – think of Spanish and Portuguese in Latin America, Russian in former Eastern Europe, German in the Austro-Hungarian empire – so the history of nationalism is one of language resistance, of battling against the language of the oppressor.

Here is P.F. Kavanagh in 1902 in an essay titled 'Ireland's Defence – Her Language' emphasising the fundamental social significance of language:

> Language marks a race of men as distinct from other races, and determines their rank among them by its antiquity, its purity, and its excellence as a means of expressing thought. The mind of a people is mirrored in their language. A people's language tells us what they were even better than their history. So true is this that even if the people had perished and their history had been lost, we might still learn from their language- and in language I include literature- to what intellectual status they had attained, what was the extent and direction of their moral development and what their general worthiness. (Kavanagh, 2000: 204–205)

Other Irish writers, of whom Brian Friel is a recent example, have written about Ireland in terms of the politics of language, and have argued that systematic attempts to suppress Irish ran up against fundamental opposition, just the Hapsburg attempt to suppress Czech ultimately failed. Czech is a fascinating case, since the Czech Revival of the 19th century that resulted in a great flowering of literature has as one of its points of origin a series of literary forgeries. Determined to break the stranglehold of German, Czech intellectuals invented an illusory period of ancient

Czech literary greatness, claiming to have discovered lost manuscripts and in the process boosted national self-confidence in quite extraordinary ways. In short, the discovery of a presumed ancient Czech literary tradition provided the spur for contemporary writers to experiment with the language that the Austrians had sought to suppress.

Similarly, the forgery by James Macpherson of the poems of the ancient Celtic bard Ossian was hugely significant in Scotland and across Europe, where Ossian rapidly acquired cult and then canonical status in those societies engaged in struggles to establish a national identity, despite the vitriol poured over the poems by such English establishment figures as Dr Johnson and Boswell. And here we come to a point that is worth noting: the importance of translation in nationalist movements. It may seem like a paradox, but the more a culture struggles to assert its own individuality and establish its own literature, to make its own voice heard, the more likely it is that translation will play a major part in the process. The true test of a language is to show that it can take the foreign, the different and the other and transform it into something familiar. It is significant that Martin Luther talked not about *übersetzen* but about *verdeutschen*, 'germanising', and that the great English Renaissance translators claimed that they were engaged in a process of 'englishing'. The importance of translation at crucial moments in time is clear: the emergence of literatures in the evolving vernacular languages of early medieval Europe is marked by translation, the road to the Reformation is filled with translations of sacred texts, the Renaissance is a time of intense translation activity and the age of revolutions in Europe and the Americas is similarly an age of translations.

Yet, even as we talk in such grandiose terms, we should not forget the role of the translator, that individual who transposes a work from one language into another. Translators translate for all kinds of reasons, not by any means always on account of national pride. Some do it for love, some for money, some out of a desire to make unknown writers come to life for new readers, some out of a crusading spirit of zealotry, some to innovate and extend the boundaries of their own literary models and some because of a particular passion for a language or an author or a work or a culture.

Translation theory has devoted little attention in recent years to the pragmatics of translation and to the subjectivity of the translator as a factor in the translation process. There is a lot of interesting research to be done here, which brings together the personal and the political. Let me offer two examples: Scotland has a particularly strong tradition of innovative translation, arguably today much stronger than England. John Corbett argues that it is the lack of a standard variety of language in Scotland that allows the translator greater possibilities, at once representing both the familiar and the strange:

> In translations into Scots we reinvent our own 'imaginary geography' in a medium which allows no invisibility to the translator. The absence of a fixed standard variety necessitates the continual reinvention of the language of the Scottish nation. (Corbett, 1999: 185)

Translation in such a context, Corbett argues, becomes a powerful means of exploring the range of a language and extending the boundaries of a literature. Crucial to such an exploration is the ability to shift perspective, to look simultaneously from within and from without, to question oneself and one's own culture as much as one questions the other. It is a view not unlike that proposed by the great Brazilian translator Augusto de Campos, who sees translation as a metamorphic process, whereby the translator enters into the skin of another being:

> Translation for me is a *persona*. Nearly a heteronym. It is to get into the pretender's skin to re-pretend everything again, each pain, each sound, each colour. This is why I never set out to translate everything. Only what I feel. (Augusto de Campos, 1998: 186)

These are different yet connected views of translation: Corbett stresses the significance of translation as a means not only of enriching a literature in a state of transition, but also as a means of reminding Scottish readers of the way in which their identity is linked to issues of language. De Campos similarly draws attention to the need for a translator to shift ground and to be open to different perspectives. Translation for him is a process of shape-changing, of re-imagining an Other. It is also an intensely personal experience, and hence his insistence on his right to be selective about what he translates. Both notions of translation hinge on the case of rejoicing in difference, rather than seeking to erase it.

Sometimes, though, a translator translates something because through the process of translating he or she finds a clue to their own identity. Such is the case with two English versions of the great Portuguese epic, *The Lusiads*, written by Luis Vaz de Camoens (*c*. 1524–1580) and published in 1572. It is an epic poem, written in ottava rima in 10 cantos, and tells the story of Vasco Da Gama's voyage of discovery to India. Camoens came from a minor aristocratic family, connected to the da Gama family. His father was a ship's captain, and perhaps unsurprisingly Camoens too was drawn to the sea, though after university he spent several years frequenting court circles and writing poetry. Romantic myths about his life abound, since he appears to have been banished from Lisbon following a duel over a woman, and sailed to India in 1553, not as an officer but as a common soldier. He returned 17 years later in 1570, having created his great epic, a hymn of praise to Portuguese seamanship and bravery and a panegyric to the Portuguese imperial ideal.

But the poem that has since become Portugal's archetypal literary masterpiece initially made little impact on Camoens' contemporaries. Moreover, the poem was already a nostalgic plea for the continuation of a greatness that was fading, as the fortunes of the Portuguese maritime empire were in decline. Then, in 1578, barely six years after *The Lusiads* appeared, came one of the greatest military disasters of the European Renaissance. The young king Sebastian led an expedition to invade Morocco, inspired by ideals of Christian crusading. At the battle of Alcaçer-Kebir, the Portuguese army was wiped out and only 100 men returned to their homeland from the 20,000 who had accompanied Sebastian into battle. The death of the king, the devastating loss of so many men, killed or enslaved devastated Camoens. Plague swept through Lisbon a few months after the terrible news from Morocco and Camoens wrote to friends from his death-bed stating that he had lost all will to survive and all hope in the future. He died in poverty on 10 June 1580, just before Philip II of Spain took over the Portuguese throne and annexed Portugal to Spain.

The Lusiads is a text that a translator approaches in different ways. On the one hand, it is an epic poem in ottava rima, not a form that sits comfortably with English, unless one thinks of Byron's brilliant use of it as an ironic form in *Don Juan*. It is a poem that has canonical status in Portuguese literature, a poem that, because of its imperial theme and the complex history of Portuguese imperial ambitions from the 16th to the 20th century has been the object of highly controversial interpretations at different points in time. Moreover, the life of Camoens himself has become a kind of frame through which subsequent generations of readers approach the poem. Knowing what happened to the author, and knowing also of the destruction of Portuguese power at Alcaçer-Kebir adds an extra dimension to a reading of this poem that sets the greatness of Vasco Da Gama's explorations together with a vision of an idealised heroic future.

The first translation of this poem into English was made by Sir Richard Fanshawe in 1655. Fanshawe was a Royalist who, during the period of the English Commonwealth in the 1650s was sent first as ambassador to Spain from 1650 to 1651 and then as ambassador to Lisbon. After the Restoration in 1660 he returned as ambassador to Spain, where he died in 1669. His translations from Spanish, Latin and Portuguese have recently been edited by Peter Davidson and it is clear that the translation of *The Lusiads*, or *Portugal's Historical Poem* in 1655 was a major undertaking, written at great speed and apparently completed within a year (Davidson, 1999). What, we may ask, inspired a courtier-turned diplomat who translated relatively little to take on such a complex task?

The answer seems to be that Fanshawe saw in the poem and in the vicissitudes and twists of fate in Camoens' life and fortunes a reflection of his own uneven fortunes. Here was a poem dedicated to a young king, a poem about past greatness and hopes for a renewal of greatness in the future. Fanshawe must have seen parallels between the world of the poem and England under Cromwell, a country waiting for the restitution of the monarch. And there is another dimension too that is worth pondering: Portugal had regained her independence from Spain in 1640, and it is not difficult to presume that Fanshawe would have seen this as a further sign of hope. Like Camoens, he had been exiled from his country and his king, like Camoens he could use a literary text to send a message to that king of hopes of future greatness, drawing upon similarities between Portugal's maritime empire and England's. Unlike Camoens, however, he had seen the restoration of Portugal's independence and implicit in his translating there must have been a sense of the inevitability of the restoration of the monarchy in England.

There are also strong personal reasons why Sir Richard Burton (1821–1891) best known for his translations from Arabic and Persian should also have translated Camoens' poem. Burton, however, was not waiting for the restoration of a king, but was waiting for his own restoration. Despite the best efforts of his wife, Burton was consistently sent on diplomatic postings that nobody else wanted, to Fernando Po, known as 'the Foreign Office graveyard', to the then under-developed Brazil, eventually to Trieste, a beautiful city but by no means a politically significant posting for a man who wanted to shape the destiny of his country. Burton considered himself hard done-by, and nurtured strong feelings of resentment to figures of authority throughout his life, resentment that led him to behaviour that hardly guaranteed him friends. He was sent down from Oxford without a degree for challenging the pronunciation of ancient Greek of his tutors, and for the rest of his life he refused to conform.[1]

His translation of *The Lusiads* was published in two volumes in 1880, followed in 1881 by another two volumes of commentary and essays on Camoens and his work (Burton, 1880, 1881). The translation has a prefatory poem by Gerald Massey in the form of a dedication. In this poem, Massey compares Burton not so much with Camoens but to Da Gama himself, the subject of *The Lusiads*:

> A man of men; a master of affairs,
> Whose own life-story is, in touching ruth,
> Poem more potent than all feigned truth.
> His Epic trails a glory in the wake
> Of *Gama, Raleigh, Frobisher* and *Drake.*
> The poem of Discovery! Sacred to
> Discoverers, and their deeds of derring-do,
> Is fitly rendered, in the Traveller's land,
> By one o' the foremost of the fearless band. (Gerald Massey, dedicatory poem in Burton, 1880).

Burton is depicted as a traveller from the land of travellers, that is England, a discoverer in the long line of explorers from Vasco Da Gama, Martin Frobisher, Raleigh and Drake. His translation is thus a means of filtering Portuguese greatness through English greatness, with himself playing a starring role: not only the translator, on this occasion, but one of the protagonists, a modern Vasco Da Gama. The first lines of the poem play with the term Burton used to describe his translation: not 'translating' but 'Englishing', a deliberate echoing of the term used by English Renaissance translators. Burton's choice of this word emphasises his own identification with the material of the text, besides reinforcing his patriotic stance.

> 'Englished by Richard Burton.' And well done,
> As it was well worth doing;

Burton claimed to know 38 languages and to dream in 17 of them. His favourite was Arabic, and he wrote his most lyrical books in praise of Arabia. He, too, grew up multilingual, educated in France before the dismal period at Oxford, whereas Fanshawe had a classical education and learned Portuguese later in life. Each of them would have answered Steiner's question about the inmost language differently, but each would have certainly understood what he meant by asking it in the first place. Exiled in different ways, Fanshawe and Burton used translation as a means of relating both to the world they inhabited and to the world they wished to inhabit in their imagination. Identity, they would both have said, is not a fixed concept. Fanshawe the diplomat, Burton the explorer and wandering consul represented England to others but were estranged from the very state that employed them. Translation offered them a vital liminal space where they could be neither one thing nor the other, neither here not there. It is the state that Eva Hoffman has written about so beautifully in her autobiographical *Lost in Translation*, a state in which the dissolving of language boundaries, the process of loss becomes the means of finding oneself (Hoffman, 1989). This is the paradox of those who exist in more than one language: to be plural and not singular. Today, in the 21st century we should not regret the lack of singularity, but rather celebrate this plurality in which millions of people now live.

Note

1. For information on the extraordinary career of Richard Burton, see Frank McLynn (1990).

The 2000 Threlford Lecture first published in *The Linguist* 39 (3), 2000.

Chapter 2
Original Sin

Word for word or sense for sense is the question facing translators. When should we follow a source text so closely that we reproduce each word, and when should we diverge from that close following to create something that effectively translates the meaning, or the sense, instead? Most translators would immediately opt for the second option, being all too aware of the pitfalls of the word-for-word approach. After all, a translation that is too literal can be simply unreadable.

Inexperienced translators seem to go for word-for-word renderings, and it seems to be a universal truth that translation in the tourist industry worldwide is pretty dire. Here are a couple of word-for-word items, one from an Indonesian hotel brochure and the other from a pamphlet produced by the city of Salamanca tourist office:

> This building is surrounded by the density of trees away from the noise of the traffic, although sometime the voice of traditional fruit sellers offering their commodity break your serenity, however it reflects the atmosphere of uniqueness.

> The characteristic feature of this building is its baldachin-style cupola which appears to hover over the central auditorium, seemingly 'turning on' the cascade of light that pours in through the lantern that crowns it.

From both these paragraphs we get an idea of what is being described, although the obscurity of expression is due to the translator having adhered too closely to the original even, in the case of the Spanish, down to translating inverted commas. In neither case has the translator felt confident enough to break away from the structures of the original so as to write a good, clear piece of English prose which, after all, is what the tourist needs. Sometimes, though, translations are so bad that the meaning is completely obscured. With so many examples of the inadequacies of literal translation everywhere we go, it is hardly surprising that many translators are wary of it.

The early development of computer translation is another example of the pitfalls of literal translation. The idea, back in the Cold War days, was that newspapers circulating in Moscow could be read in Washington simultaneously, thanks to the skills of computer translation programs. Here too, literal translation proved a reef on which that kind of linguistic idealism foundered. Languages are in a constant state of movement, and the early computer programmes, which were glorified dictionaries, missed whole dimensions of language use, particularly the figurative. If I translate a phrase such as 'the onset of darkness', the context will tell me whether 'darkness' is being used literally or figuratively, that is, to indicate a state of mind. If it is being used figuratively, then depending on the language into which I am translating, I will have to use a different word from that which renders the physical condition of nightfall. In short, I will have to think through a set of textual and contextual problems, and the early computers did not think like that at all. These days, computer translation is a sophisticated enterprise, and the old weaknesses of literality just a distant memory. Nevertheless, the inadequacy of machine translation in dealing with certain kinds of text opened up debates about forms of translation that still continue.

So with all this in mind, why would anyone want to defend literal translation? Can it ever be useful? Well, yes, it can. Literal translation has long been used in language learning as a means of testing grammatical and semantic competence, or incompetence, as the case may be. My son recently produced a German sentence that read: *Ich bin lesen ein gut Buch*. Apart from having remembered to capitalise the noun, he had managed to create an aberration. His defence, of course, was that he had translated literally: I am = *Ich bin*, reading = *lesen*, a = *ein*, good = *gut*, book = *Buch*. I protested that he had failed to take an account of the use of the present continuous in English and the presence of case endings in German. This, of course, is where I discovered the impossibility of explaining grammatical error to a generation that has no vocabulary with which to talk about grammar, but I will not go into that here for fear of exposing myself as a reactionary, antediluvian, grammarian with a deep distrust of the conversational method of language teaching. All I will say is that after some discussion, the difference between the English and German sentence began to emerge, and through the errors of literal translation he was able to see an alternative. My mantra repeated to all my children and students over the years that what is wonderful about knowing other languages is that you can do different things in different ways in different languages seemed to have been heard. Literal translation can operate as a first step in a process of acquiring skills that involve thinking in a new way and trying to interpret the world differently, through understanding how another language works.

A book by Robert Stanton, *The Culture of Translation in Anglo-Saxon England*, sheds new light on the importance of literal translation in the development of the English vernacular. Until I read this, I had not considered the importance of literal translation as a tool for people speaking a vernacular language to develop their own written version. English emerged in a written form in the Anglo-Saxon period when some of the flourishing oral literature began to appear in manuscript. The earliest English texts were interlinear glosses of Latin writings, mostly religious works. The glosses were notes on the text, written either between the lines or in the margins, and often they were literal translations of Latin words or phrases. The complexity of glossing systems has been the subject of several scholarly studies, but for the purposes of this essay, let us think of glosses as a form of literal translation. The function of glossing was clearly to enable readers to understand the Latin work.

In the 7th century AD, the Venerable Bede proposed that the Lord's Prayer and the Apostles' Creed should be translated into English, both for the common people and 'for clerics or monks who are unskilled in the Latin language'. This suggests that monks were by no means as skilled in Latin as might have been supposed. The Anglo-Saxon world was not one in which learning could flourish easily. Apart from restricted supplies of manuscripts, scribes to copy them and teachers to disseminate knowledge, not all rulers promoted learning, and disease, wars and Viking raiders made consistent study difficult. In that world, translating literally and commenting on the Latin works that were available became a way of disseminating knowledge relatively easily. Two tasks could be fulfilled by such a translation exercise: the person writing the glossary would become better acquainted with the structures of Latin, and the knowledge contained in the Latin text would be made available to people whose knowledge of Latin was weak.

Stanton suggests that Anglo-Saxon literary culture 'was indelibly marked by the very idea of translation'. Through literal translation, understanding spread and gradually Anglo-Saxon began to acquire status in its own right as a written language. By the time of King Alfred (849–899), it was possible for the king to introduce bilingual education to England and to state, as he does in his preface to one of his own translations, that translation is necessary so that 'all the free born youths who are now in England, who have the means to apply themselves to it, be set to learning, whenever they have no other duties, until the time that they can read English writing well'. Then, Alfred declares that those whom teachers wish to educate further can begin to learn Latin as well.

The story of literal translation through interlinear glossing of early manuscripts is not just a specialised tale for scholars, but the story of the birth of written English. Similarly, interlinear glossing in other European languages gave rise to other written forms of vernacular, and meant that oral literature that had circulated for centuries, such as the great Germanic epics, the songs, riddles and stories could be set down in languages that, at the very least, could stand up to Latin, even if they could not outdo Latin stylistically at that point in time.

It is interesting to reflect on the role of literal translation in the development of language skills. I started out disparaging word-for-word versions, and I would still argue that a good translation moves on beyond the literal, but close rendering of a text serves a very definite purpose.

The scribes making their Anglo-Saxon jottings were, one trusts, much better linguists than my son, but the principle of aligning words so as to understand how different languages work is one that is still recognisable over centuries.

First published in *ITI Bulletin* May–June 2004.

Chapter 3
Theory and Practice: The Old Dilemma

Translation theory has never been so popular. New books appear all the time, conferences are constantly advertised and PhD theses abound. Research in the field of translation is flourishing to such an extent that there are now different schools of thought, pursuing different goals and staking out their own particular territory.

But how much does all this research, some of it very exciting, some of it, frankly, dull and at its worst, impenetrably obscure, affect translators? Do the people who sit down and engage with the activity of translating benefit from what the theorists are doing, or do they largely ignore it? Equally important is the question put the other way round: to what extent do translation theorists engage with the experience of translators and how are their theories shaped by what happens in practice?

The divide between theory and practice is a particularly British phenomenon, but it should not be underestimated. It exists in all sorts of disciplines, at its most obvious where there is a practical dimension to a subject such as theatre, fine art, music or writing. How many times have I heard practitioners tell me that they do not need theory, they just need to get on with the job and be creative! The more you talk about something, their anti-theory line goes, the further away from the authenticity that only practice conveys.

Yet, the division is not really a division at all, for practitioners do talk about their work and can often articulate what they do and how they do it very well indeed. The problem is one of language, or rather discourse, for theory is seen as an intellectualising process, with its own language and rules that have to be learned, and many practitioners feel inhibited by what they perceive as obscurantism. It has been put to me that theorists patronise translators, who are, after all, engaged in very high level, complex intellectual activity. Translating, as Gabriel Garcia Marquez (2002) so succinctly puts it, is not only the best and most rigorous kind of reading, it is also of all literary activities the most difficult, the least recognised and the worst paid. Translators can be forgiven for feeling not a little aggrieved with their status in the world.

Right now in the field of translation, a number of theorists have been proclaiming the importance of the translator's role. Translators as individuals have played a crucial part in the transmission of literary works and ideas, yet they have often been more or less invisible. With greater emphasis being placed on the importance of the translator, the visibility of the translator has therefore become a key idea in current translation theory. Lawrence Venuti's (1995) book titled *The Translator's Invisibility* made a good case for the importance of the translator, showing how translators had actively restructured works in the target language despite being seen as little more than transparent filters through which words passed almost by alchemy.

So do translators appreciate Venuti's efforts on their behalf? From talking to several people who have read his book and admired his scholarship, the verdict is mixed. Of course, practitioners appreciate the efforts he has made to promote the cause of translation, but there is some disquiet about one of Venuti's ideas that has been much discussed in theoretical circles; the problem of what he calls 'foreignization' as opposed to 'domestication' or, as others term it, 'acculturation' (Venuti, 1995). All these are trendy terms right now, and positions on the relative merits of these different translation strategies vary considerably.

I hope Venuti (who is a friend) will forgive me if I attempt a summary of his ideas on foreignisation. Briefly, Venuti is suggesting that translators should somehow highlight the foreignness of the texts they translate, so as to ensure that readers recognise that they are reading a work that originated somewhere else in some other culture. If a translation erases all traces of the foreign, he argues, the translator will indeed become invisible and besides, the foreign texts will be appropriated by the receiving culture and its intrinsic other qualities will disappear.

This is not an original theory: Venuti closely follows the thinking of the German Romantic, Friedrich Schleiermacher, whose ideas on translation were formulated in the early 19th century, in opposition to the French school of thinking about translation which cheerfully domesticated everything, so that ancient Greek heroes were visualised as courtiers at Versailles. Nevertheless, Venuti's theory of foreignisation as a translation strategy struck a chord among post-colonial scholars of translation who have been perturbed by domesticating translations that erase all trace of foreignness.

Some of the translators who have expressed anxiety about foreignisation, however, approach the question very differently. They know about markets, they know what readers want and they know that most readers want a readable, accessible book that reads easily and fluently. What they do not want are books that are difficult to read, full of strange words and difficult phrases, and above all they do not want translations that read like translations. In consequence, politically incorrect or not, most good translators want to produce works that are going to be read, and they want to write well.

Gregory Rabassa, one of the world's greatest translators, acknowledges that nobody can reproduce the structure of another language in a translation without creating gibberish. Nevertheless, he argues, 'there ought to be some undercurrent, some background hum' that enables a reader to see that translation does not happen by magic (Rabassa, 2002: 89–90). The task of the translator in his view is to negotiate the delicate passage between the shoals of obscurantism and the reefs of complacency. The translator, for Rabassa must be modest, then must be careful and cannot impose himself, and yet, he must be adventurous and original, bound all the while to someone else's thoughts and words. In this sense, translation is a baroque art, one where the structure is foreordained but where the second artist must decorate it according to the lights of his own culture. His genius is secondhand, in a sense, but he still has a chance to strut his stuff within the limits before him.

Here is a practitioner theorising about translation, and in so doing coming up with the wonderful image of baroque art. It is notable that Rabassa talks about a first and second artist, acknowledging the artistry of translation while recognising that the translator is always necessarily constrained by the fact that there is an original that supplies the primary material for the translation.

Some of the most useful theorising about translation has come from practitioners. Percy Bysshe Shelley's concept of translation as organic transplantation is one of my favourite images, as is Octavio Paz' (1992) idea that while a writer fixes words into a perfect form, the task of the translator is to liberate those same words and free them into another language where they will feel at home. What many practitioners do not like, however, are theorists proposing models for translation to which they are expected to adhere, without regard for the broader picture – for the expectations of target readers, the pressures of the market and the literary tradition of a culture.

In 2002, serving as one of the judges for the Independent Foreign Fiction Prize, we shortlisted a novel translated from French by Adriana Hunter; entitled $9.99. It was not a great novel, and its author, Frederic Beighbeder (2000), is far less well known than his contemporary who writes in a similar vein, the highly controversial Michel Houllebecq. But the reason why we felt that this translation deserved commendation was because of the translator's skill in domesticating a French work. For Hunter transposed every Parisian reference to London, found an equivalent English advertising slogan for every French one, tracked down the trendiest restaurants and boutiques and wine-bars in London and substituted every French reference. She effectively erased the French context in which the novel was set, and yet the narrative that involved ghastly cocaine-fuelled advertising people worked in its new context. This was an incredibly risky strategy for a translator, but which we could not help admiring. Only last week a friend rang me to tell me how great she thought the novel was – she had not realised that it was a translation.

But if the greatest compliment a reader can pay is for a translation not to seem like a translation, this means that translation theory with its emphasis on otherness and its concern to stress the downside of domestication is somewhat out of step with translation practice. The question I ask myself is whether we have entered a new phase, and whether translation theory needs to engage more openly with translators. Perhaps readers have views on this: the debate has only just begun.

First published in *ITI Bulletin* November–December 2003.

Chapter 4
Dangerous Translations

A short report in a newspaper recently caught my attention. Several bodies had been found in Afghanistan, all victims of the Taliban. They had been brutally murdered and their tongues cut out, whether before or after death was not stated. All had been working as interpreters.

This is not the first newspaper report of the torture and murder of interpreters and translators, particularly in Iraq and Afghanistan, but was by far the most shocking. Some countries, such as Denmark, have provided safe havens for those interpreters in danger of their lives who have worked with allied forces in Iraq, and a trawl through websites shows that there are some organisations that are showing concern for the plight of interpreters caught up in conflict zones. But most of the time, to judge by the small amount of coverage in the media, the risks encountered by translators and interpreters in carrying out their daily tasks are rarely ever mentioned. Even this appalling story received very little media attention.

There is a paradox here: on the one hand, translators seem to be invisible to most of the world, yet they are also seen by some to be so important that their very lives are under threat. The men who murdered the Afghan interpreters so brutally clearly saw themselves as executing criminals; yet what crime does an interpreter commit when he or she gets on with the job of facilitating communication between people who would not otherwise be able to understand one another?

There is no easy answer to this question, for it leads us along pathways into dark areas of unconscious fears of Otherness, which threaten our sense of identity and the security we want to feel by being in control of the world through language. Stories abound of people feeling threatened when they cannot understand what is being said. I have encountered many such tales, ranging from someone who said that he felt he was going to be subjected to violence when a small group gathered around him in an Asian market, to someone feeling that she was being maligned by neighbours who deliberately spoke in Welsh when she went into her local village post office. All these stories have features in common: not being able to understand what is being said in another language stirs feelings of anxiety, which are quickly translated into feelings of being threatened. It is, of course, entirely possible that the group who gathered round the man in the bazaar were not talking about him at all, or that the Welsh-speaking neighbours were exchanging news that had nothing to do with the English incomer, but the point is that, that is not how they perceived these situations. From not understanding the language, they leapt immediately to negative conclusions.

Nothing creates a stronger sense of Us versus Them than mutual linguistic incomprehension, and hence the huge importance of interpreters, people who can bridge the divide and help promote greater understanding. But given that tensions can arise through linguistic differences in everyday situations such as buying goods in a market or a village post office, it is obvious that in situations of highly charged political or military conflicts, those tensions will be increased, which means that the role played by bilinguals can quickly become a very dangerous role indeed.

The language we use to talk about translation reflects that sense of anxiety. We often refer to translators as occupying a 'no-man's land', which summons up images of trench warfare. This raises the question as to whether translators do indeed belong to one side or the other, and in real wartime situations it can be a small step to viewing translators as collaborators, using language in order to betray their own people. For images of betrayal also feature strongly in how we talk about translation. There is the famous Italian adage, *traduttore/traditore* which plays on the fact that the word for translator is so close to the word for traitor, and the notion of the translator as a turncoat exists in many cultures.

Being suspicious of translators and interpreters is by no means a modern phenomenon. The history of the translation of sacred texts such as the Bible is, from one perspective, a history of violence and bloodshed. Translators who endeavoured to create vernacular versions of the Bible were often persecuted and even put to death. The bitter battles over English translations of the Bible led to the death of that great translator, William Tyndale at the stake in 1536. Tyndale's predecessor, John Wycliffe died before the authorities could execute him, but his bones were dug up and burned in 1395, and the unfortunate Czech theologian, Jan Hus, whose work was influenced by Wycliffe, was first burned at the stake in 1415, after which his bones were burned and the ashes scattered in the sea. Henry VIII complained bitterly that translating the Bible into English would lead to 'that most precious jewel, the work of God' being 'disputed, rhymed, sung and jangled in every alehouse and tavern' in the land.

Contemporary translators have also good cause to fear religious extremists. The German scholar who translated the Koran in 2000 was interviewed in the *ITI Bulletin* in the November/December 2008 issue about why he had felt it necessary to publish under a pseudonym. This had become necessary following the fatwa issued against Salman Rushdie that led to the murder of his Japanese translator in 1991 and to attacks on the Italian and Norwegian translators of Rushdie's novel, *The Satanic Verses*. Rushdie himself, as is well known, spent years in hiding.

Language is powerful. There is an old English saying which goes like 'sticks and stones may break my bones, but words will never hurt me.' This is simply nonsense. Words can wound more sharply than knives, and as can be seen by the death threats issued to translators through the ages, translation whether of a written text or oral interpretation can be punishable by death in some contexts.

For the fact is that whenever a translation is required, this means that individuals are not able to communicate with one another without help from someone with knowledge of that other language, and this means taking on trust not only the expertise but also the honesty of the person translating. This can be difficult: only the other day I was in the car listening to the radio, to an interview with Pakistani flood victims and heard a woman say a few sentences that were then rendered into a speech lasting a good two minutes in English, a speech that contained not only information about the plight of the woman and her family but also about the need for more international aid to be sent to the flood victims. I was left with doubt about what had actually been translated, for though the humanitarian message was clear and important, it was hard to believe that a few sentences spoken by a peasant woman in a rural village could have become an impassioned plea for international aid articulated in over a dozen English sentences. Even accepting that this was a radio programme and therefore editing was a factor to be counted, the disparity between the length of the utterance of the Pakistani speaker and the length of the interpreter's speech was troubling. How much more troubling might such disparities be in a context where there is distrust on both sides from the start?

We have always needed translators and interpreters, especially in times of conflict and international antagonisms. Wars are fought with weapons, but peace treaties are made with words, and without men and women who seek to diffuse tensions and misunderstandings by bringing the enlightenment of mutual comprehension to the table the shaping of such treaties would be impossible. The brutal murder of the Afghan interpreters serves to show us all how vital interlingual communication is if we want to create a better world, and how badly we all need brave people capable of facilitating that communication. The risks they take are huge, because they are dealing not only with the hostilities of a particular conflict, but with deep-seated psychological fears of Otherness, fears that stem from the terrible power of a language that is unknown to us, outside of us and belonging to other people who may be our enemies. Translators and interpreters who have the courage to face down those fears in their day-to-day work deserve our respect and admiration.

First published in *ITI Bulletin* November–December 2010.

Chapter 5

How Modern Should Translations Be?

I have been reading some Victorian translators who tended to favour the use of a strange archaic English, like no English that has ever been written before full of 'yet' and 'yea' and 'verily' and tongue-twisting compounds. This was clearly the popular language of the day, and regardless of whether an original was in ancient Greek or in Sanskrit, it would appear in mock-medieval English. But tastes change, and fake medievalism is now perceived as quaintly comical, and so those translations have disappeared from view, probably forever.

What is interesting, though, is that it should have lasted so long. The history of translation, like any other kind of writing, can tell us a lot about the tastes of a particular culture at a particular time, and the medieval world, fake or not, exerted a strong pull on readers whose daily reality was coloured by the expanding cities and grimy factories of industrial Victorian England. Today, in contrast, we favour translating into modern English, into a language that is accessible to most readers.

But this in turn raises the question of how far a translator can go. How modern can you be? For language is in a perpetual state of transformation, and some languages, of which English is one, change very rapidly indeed. New words come into fashion, change their meaning and disappear. My 14-year-old praises things by saying they are 'sweet' or 'wick-ed', with the accent on the second syllable. A 'wick-ed' film is not an abomination, but one he really enjoyed. I hear 'bad' used in the same way, that is, to mean 'good'. That was 'well bad' is a phrase often heard in our house, meaning that something was really good.

Slang, particularly teenage slang or workplace slang, has always changed quickly. Lexicographers have trouble keeping up, and every new edition of the *Oxford English Dictionary* contains words that have not been in previous editions, words that are often then debated in the media. Twenty years ago, nobody talked about being 'hassled', and today it is commonplace. Where societies undergo radical changes, as happened across Europe after the collapse of communism, languages change radically too. I have no Arabic, but I am sure that everyday language in Iraq is changing at a much faster pace than it did during the static years of dictatorship. Social change and linguistic change are interconnected, and this can affect translators in two ways.

First, translators are under pressure to make a work available to contemporary readers but they need to decide what kind of contemporary language to use. Ali G's English may be funny now, but it will not be funny in the very near future, it will seem as dated as the language of Evelyn Waugh's Oxford undergraduates in *Brideshead Revisited*.

Second, they may be translating a work that was considered radically modern in its own time, and hence the pressure to find an equivalent way of signalling modernity becomes even greater. Granted, Aristophanes was an ancient Greek playwright, but in his day he was a satirist who could touch the nerve-centre of his own society. Should a translator of his plays opt for modern English only, or go even further and try to find parallels for Aristophanes' political jokes in contemporary society? Often, translators of plays go for the latter choice, producing very funny versions that are filled with meaning in the here and now. But the problem is that such translations date very quickly, and constantly need revision. It is an interesting fact that play translations date more quickly than other forms of translation, and this must be linked to the immediacy of the spoken language employed by a translator and, in some cases, to the ephemeral quality of the references.

Some translators have argued that if a work is ancient or medieval, the translator should signal its antiquity in some way in the language of the translation. This was the Victorian view, but the main reason that the vogue for medievalising died out is that translators were having to invent a language, for nobody ever spoke the fake medieval English many of them used in their written versions, and the result was unconvincing to readers.

My own view is that if a translation is going to sound authentic and be readable, the translator must write in his or her own language, in a language rooted in reality, not fantasy.

Where modernising becomes especially problematic is when a decision is taken to update sacred texts prayers in particular. I recently went to three churches in one week. The Catholic congregation knew all the prayers by heart and said them at a speed that can only come with complete familiarity with the words. Yet, there were members of the congregation who had grown up with the Latin Mass, and had had to relearn prayers taught in childhood. In an Anglican cathedral, the congregation likewise knew all the responses by heart, but in one small Anglican church I visited, the order of service was handed to us on a printed sheet, and the congregation appeared confused. When the Lord's Prayer was said, half the congregation, myself included, recited the prayer we knew of old; the others read a differently worded prayer off the printed sheet. Two English languages resounded round the church.

The case of modernising has been passionately made. A church that fails to move with the times, linguistically and in other ways, it is argued, will lose ground and alienate a younger generation. But the case has perhaps not been convincingly made, for only certain elements of the service, from what I could see, have been changed into more modern English, and even that supposedly modern variety is still a long way away from everyday speech. I found myself wondering too, why it is that though prayers may be modernised, hymns are not. Football supporters cheerfully sing 'Abide with me' on the terraces, but that's hardly modern English. Just for fun, I tried translating the first verse into the kind of English the football fans might use. The original hymn, by H.F. Lyte (1793–1847), runs like this:

> Abide with me; fast falls the eventide:
> The darkness deepens; Lord with me abide!
> When other helpers fail, and comforts flee,
> Help of the helpless, O abide with me.

My version is as follows:

> Stay with me; night's coming on quickly:
> It's getting much darker; stay with me, Lord.
> When other helpers bottle out and you're really stuck,
> Help the helpless, and stay with me, will you?

I am being facetious here to make a point. Rhythm is important in hymns, and so is rhyme, and my version has neither. But rhythm is also important in prayers, and even more important is the power of a language that serves a ritual function in society. The big question that remains to be answered is whether updating the ritual language of prayer serves the desired purpose of reaching more and younger people, or whether it diminishes by appearing to trivialise that language. Do people genuinely not understand the phrase 'forgive us our trespasses', and does the phrase 'forgive us our misdeeds' fulfil the function of modernising to which it aspires? And if modernising is so important, why does it not seem to matter to the crowds who cheerfully sing hymns at sporting events?

The modernisation of language affects everybody, not only translators. We all hold strong views: some of us believe that clinging to outdated versions of texts and refusing to abandon old rules of grammar and pronunciation is an undesirable sign of being out of touch with contemporary society. Others believe that the constant coining of new jargon, the tampering with much-loved texts and the insistence on modernity is a sign of a society that has abandoned its traditional values and lost its way. The reality is probably somewhere in between those two poles. The dilemma for a translator, whose business is words, is knowing how to strike a balance between tradition and modernising, knowing when to innovate and when to leave well alone. As with so many aspects of the translator's task, it is impossible to please everyone.

First published in *ITI Bulletin* March–April 2004.

Chapter 6
Status Anxiety

It is an experience that anyone who works with different languages must have encountered: you are sitting peacefully somewhere, when someone rings/knocks on the door/comes up to you somewhere in public and asks you to translate something for them. Often what they want translated are incredibly complex legal documents, instruction manuals, scientific papers or some such thing.

I remember once sitting with friends in an idyllic village café in the Dordogne, when I was asked to translate a builder's estimate for an American expatriate's house extension, all hand written and containing technical terms I would not have understood in English. Second homes seem to bring out this impulse in people, and I can think of French papers concerning rights of way, Portuguese land disputes and Italian notary public documents that have found their way onto my desk.

The reason for this kind of behaviour can be found in society's attitudes to translation. People who do not translate or, worse still, have no acquaintance with any other language seem to assume that a translator is all-powerful. Give us a document, no matter what the subject matter, and we will transform it into an understandable English equivalent. That many of us might not understand technical terms in our own language seems to pass such people by, as does the idea that they might employ a professional translator to do a decent job.

Friends who are GPs or dentists complain of similar behaviour. They are forever being approached at parties and asked to offer a diagnosis on symptoms graphically recounted over a third glass of wine. I suppose that it is simply one of the hazards of the profession, but where translators are concerned, the situation is slightly different. Although everyone respects doctors, even when badgering them, there is a dual attitude to translators. Those people who assume that translators have the power to interpret for them are reluctant to see this skill as worth paying for, and when the same people talk about books they have read that were originally written in other languages, one can be sure that they will mention the author's name, not the name of the translator without whom they would not have been able to read the book at all.

These days I am more annoyed by the marginalisation of translators than I was when in my evangelical phase some 20 years ago. Back then, freshly scarred from some horrible experiences in the freelance translation world, I wasted no opportunity to proclaim the importance of the role of translators everywhere I went. I had come to see some of the abuses suffered by translators when translations are commissioned outside the safety net of professional organisations. On one occasion I had spent days translating a film script, only to find the producer offering only a fraction of the agreed fee because the script was not worth following up. I protested that this was not my fault but was due to the abysmal quality of the screenplay in the first place, but I only managed to get half the original fee after considerable argument. Many times my translations would appear in print without any acknowledgement, and proofs of the first book I translated arrived with the name of the author and the series editor in large print and my name in brackets much lower down the title page. I wrote a passionate letter to the publisher, who was based in New York, complaining about this, and for once my appeal was heard and my name appeared properly in the published version, but the episode taught me a lot about how translators are treated, even by reputable publishers.

Many translators in the United Kingdom who are asked to translate plays complain bitterly that their work is sneered at, before being handed over to a well-known playwright who makes minimal alterations and proclaims him- (or her-) self as the translator.

This unhappy state of affairs seems to be a peculiarly English phenomenon, and the attempts at justification by producers, who will often claim that the hand of a playwright is needed to transform a 'literal' version into a 'performable' version, remain, in my view, unethical.

Reviewers in literary journals and newspapers do not help the situation either. I recently saw reviews of Maureen Freely's translation of the latest Orhun Pamuk novel and rejoiced that both names were featured in every review I read.

This is unusual, for though newspapers like *The Independent* give due attention to the part the translator plays in bringing novels to English language readers, even to the extent of sponsoring an annual fiction in translation prize, most reviewers ignore the translator. Even where translators' names are mentioned, the reviewer will often discuss the novel as though it had not been translated at all.

In some cases, translations are published without the name of the translator appearing anywhere. One of the entries for the 2003 *Independent*

Foreign Fiction Prize was submitted by a publisher who had omitted to list the translator. Needless to say, it did not make the shortlist.

But this state of affairs continues also because of the ambiguous attitude of many translators towards their role. Many translators do not want publicity, they do not want to be featured as prominently as original authors and they see their role as one of facilitating rather than creating. In this respect, translators can perhaps be compared with teachers or nurses who do not aspire to the public prominence coveted by many professors or hospital consultants and are content instead to do a good, professional job out of the glare of publicity.

The desire for invisibility on the part of many translators takes us to the heart of the matter.

Recently, I wrote a piece that described translation as craftsmanship. I was reprimanded by a translator friend who insisted that I should have described translation as an art instead. On this point, we had an obvious misunderstanding, for by highlighting the craft involved in translating, the intention was to praise the skill of the translator rather than to denigrate achievement.

That translation may be a creative activity does not mean that it is not also a craft, just as furniture making or fashion designing are both craftwork and creative. The issue underlying our disagreement was terminological, but as with any dispute about language, there is always a deeper layer of significance. In this case, the issue was one of perception, for he felt that to describe translation as a craft was to diminish its importance.

Perhaps, in a world obsessed with labels, he is right in insisting on using language that reinforces the importance and the status of translation. Nevertheless, many translators are happy with the idea of craftsmanship in translation, which carries connotations of a long apprenticeship served and a deep understanding of primary materials which the expert translator can then shape as he or she thinks fit. The primary material that the translator uses is, of course, language.

Interestingly, although theatre practitioners in many countries talk about the 'art' or even about the 'science' of theatre, few would do so in English, where, more pragmatically, they tend to talk about the 'work', thereby avoiding the art or craft debate altogether.

Regardless of terminological disputes or the desire of many translators to remain quietly invisible as they get on with the job of translating the text in hand, it is important for those of us who work with translation to reinforce the message of the importance of translators in the world we inhabit. Translation may not be as highly regarded as it should be; it is still poorly and often erratically paid, and people still have misconceptions about what it entails, but if every translator on the planet were to disappear overnight, the world would be in an even worse mess than it is now.

I still feel it is my duty to preach the gospel of the importance of translation, in hopes that some of the monolingual unconverted will hear it and respond.

First published in *ITI Bulletin* September–October 2004.

Chapter 7
Under the Influence

Reading a literary review the other day, my attention was caught by a phrase used by the reviewer. The author in question, he wrote, had been influenced by several sources, and he went on to list three or four writers that, in his opinion, had been the inspiration behind the author's work. Since those writers were from different countries and had written their works in different languages, I started thinking about the idea of influence and wondered how the reviewer could be so certain. Unless the writer he was discussing had access to those languages, any influence that may have taken place must surely have happened through translation which, however, was never mentioned.

When I was an undergraduate studying comparative literature, there was something loosely identified as 'influence studies'. Some critics saw the tracing of influences as central to any literary comparison, while others argued that proving influence was quite impossible. What nobody seemed to discuss, however, was the relevance of translation here. For although in some cases it is clear that writers had read other writers in the original, it is also clear than many of them did not. The huge impact and resulting influence on many writers of the plays of the Norwegian Ibsen and the Swedish Strindberg at the end of the 19th century owed everything to translation, since hardly anyone outside their own countries could understand Norwegian or Swedish.

In literary criticism, translation is the poor relation, which is particularly galling in a field as broad as comparative literature. Nor does translation figure as prominently as it should do in the current fashionable field of post-colonial studies. There seems to be an assumption that works of literature can pass between cultures transparently, that they can somehow seep through from one time and place into another, despite the fact that they also have to pass through a far more impermeable barrier: the barrier of language. Critics and reviewers need to take account of this stage in the transfer process, for it is absurd to claim that one writer has influenced another if no regard is taken for the complexities of linguistic transfer and the role of the translator.

If we consider literary history in broad sweeps, then what becomes obvious straightaway is the central significance of translation in the movement of writing from one context to another. Great periods of innovation and change in writing are always linked to translation in some way. Someone once said that the Reformation was primarily a dispute between translators, and of course translation was fundamental in the Renaissance also. European Romanticism spread through translation: the huge influence of Macpherson and Byron on emerging literatures in central, southern and eastern Europe was not because so many writers from those regions knew English, but because of the quality of the translations that they used as sources of inspiration. This is what happens frequently with translation: a work is translated, a new readership gains access and finds inspiration in what now appears as different, new and exciting. Writers from that new readership then set off on their own personal creative journeys, adapting what they have read in translation into their own context, acknowledging their own history and traditions. This is how the sonnet form spread rapidly across Europe, with each language adapting that very versatile form to conventions from different traditions. Earlier, this is how the great epic poems of the early Middle Ages moved and were transformed, so that Roland, the old French epic hero eventually became the protagonist of Sicilian puppet plays and the shadowy Arthur of Welsh and Breton origins became a central figure in Western iconography. It is what is happening now, in China, after years of restricted access to other literatures, and the translation boom, combined with a wealth of new writers testifies to a great surge of creativity that undoubtedly will have traces of otherness implicit in it.

Writers have always borrowed from one another, and so it could be said that influence is intrinsic to the art of writing. 'An artist cares about the perfectability of the work, and not just the fact that it may have originated from himself or from others,' wrote the polyglot Argentinian writer, Borges (2002b: 9). Wherever Shakespeare took his plots from, it is clear that translation from several languages was involved somewhere. Goethe sought inspiration from the Orient, James Joyce borrowed from everywhere. Writing in 1918, Ezra Pound (1963: 194) advised writers to 'be influenced by as many great artists as you can, but have the decency either to acknowledge the debt outright, or to try to conceal it'. Pound's witty advice is at the heart of all writing, and he, more than most writers, was profoundly aware of the importance of translation. His greatest achievement, the *Cantos* is an extraordinary tour de force, written over many years by a poet with encyclopaedic knowledge of world literature and a hunger to read more in languages he did not know.

Shortly before the First World War, working with other artists, Pound devised the idea of a creative source of energy which they called a vortex. Instead of seeing influence as something that could be transmitted in a linear manner, from A to B, these writers proposed the idea of a great vortex of energy, through, in and from which ideas would surge about at high speed. In the rush of ideas notions of originality and derivation would dissolve, so that arguments about who had first thought of something, about sources and borrowings and copyings, about faithfulness and unfaithfulness would be eclipsed. It is an interesting image, and very much of its time, encapsulating the philosophy of an age that, with hindsight, can be seen as the start of today's globally networked world. The dominant images of today are those of networks, webs, intersections, maps and DNA models rather than a vortex, but the notion of trying to explain creative forces through scientific imagery is the same.

Pound is a particularly interesting case where ideas of influence are concerned. In 1915, he published a collection of translations titled *Cathay* based on notes by the Sinologist Ernest Fenellosa and cribs to the ideograms of Li Po. Opinion divides as to whether these poems can be defined as 'translations', although it is clear that without Fenellosa they would not have been written. To the extent that there was a process of interlinguistic transfer involved, in my view the *Cathay* poems are translations. But the success of these poems owes as much to the time when they appeared as to Pound's poetic abilities, and this is an added difficulty whenever we try to establish patterns of influence. The images of despair, sadness and loss that Pound recreated from the ancient Chinese texts struck a chord with a generation of readers appalled by the horrors of what was happening on the battlefields of the First World War. The famous 'Lament of the Frontier Guard' had a totally contemporary feel to it, as these lines show:

> I climb the towers and towers
> To watch out over the barbarous land:
> There is no wall left to this village.
> Bones white with a thousand frosts,
> High heaps, covered with trees and grass;
> Who brought this to pass?
> Who has brought the flaming imperial anger?
> Who has brought the army with drums and with kettle-drums?

Pound's *Cathay* spoke to a whole generation, so that a collection of obscure poems translated from the Chinese were transformed into a work that could be read as a lament against the cruelty and irrationality of war. Seeking to translate oriental poetry for Western readers, Pound inadvertently became known as one of the great war poets of his generation.

The importance of translation in the transmission of literature should not be underestimated and it certainly should not be ignored. Recently, with my students, we have been discussing the diverse fortunes in different countries of the works of Hans Christian Andersen, the bicentenary of whose birth falls this year. What is blindingly obvious is that without translations, this writer would never have become known outside his native country, and the extent of his fame around the world is dependent on the work of (often anonymous) translators. In Andersen's case, given the relative inaccessibility of Danish, translations were frequently made through a third language, but whatever the process, the resulting impact of one of the world's most canonical children's writers came about through the work of translators.

I would like to see the role of translation given the attention it deserves in literary studies generally. I find it bizarre that this should not have happened, for literature is made out of words and writers use words familiar to them in their own language. We seem able to accept the idea of international travel, global communication and cross-referencing and influence across cultures. What prevents us then from seeing that these transactions are, ultimately, all about translation?

First published in *ITI Bulletin*, July–August 2005.

Chapter 8
Reference Point

I once happened to mention that never a week goes by that I do not look something up in one dictionary or another. I could have added that I use my thesaurus on a daily basis too. Dictionaries of all kinds – rhyming dictionaries, bilingual dictionaries, monolingual dictionaries in various languages, concordances, the thesaurus and place name dictionaries are all basic tools of any writer's craft. Or so I thought, until I received several emails from people who told me they felt inhibited about admitting their reliance on dictionaries and thanked me for 'coming out as a dictionary-user', as it were. One very distinguished writer told me he had once been criticised and made to feel inferior by a so-called elite literary gathering at which writers who resort to dictionaries were derided as inadequate.

Last week the same story cropped again, only this time the writer affirming the fundamental importance of dictionaries as a means of developing the craft of writing was the award-winning poet and translator from Northern Ireland, Ciaran Carson (2002). In his wonderfully witty way, he argued that the problem is not with writers who feel they do have to use dictionaries all the time, but rather with those writers who think that they do not! He goes even further than I do, and looks up words on the internet, and we both agreed, as we worked with an international group of students, that anyone who thinks they are above using a dictionary has not understood that all writing, whether it involves translation or not, is a craft that needs to be refined over years, like any other, and that experience of both failure and success needs to be based on constant practice and good, well-sharpened tools. Like dictionaries!

Working in a language like English with a vast vocabulary means that there are large numbers of words that are not quite synonyms but almost. The word 'listening' is not quite the same as 'hearing', nor is the word 'glitter' the same as 'glisten', although they will be rendered in the same way in translation into languages with a more restricted vocabulary because they are almost the same. This means that English is a language that lends itself well to poetry, and also to irony and humour, for words with different shades of meanings can be used subtly and to great effect. But the sheer variety of words on offer can also cause difficulties. I have been using my dictionary a lot lately, trying to find words for the sounds of water in English. It is a tough search. I am writing poems about Scalan House, the extraordinary place in the north of Scotland that served as a seminary for the last handful of Catholic priests after the Jacobite risings were so brutally suppressed, and I want to convey something of the soundscape of the place. What you hear when you walk there is the sound of wind, water and birds and nothing else, but trying to express the sound of the burn keeps ending up in cliché. Longfellow wrote about water gushing and struggling, some poets give us laughing brooks, others go for more Latinate terms and Tennyson gave us the most famous brook of all:

> I chatter over stony ways
> In little sharps and trebles,
> I bubble into eddying bays,
> I babble on the pebbles.

I want something that will give a sense of the sound of water, but will recognise also the solemnity of the place. I need a word for what the stream does that will pair with another line, 'the hiss of grass in the wind', where the word 'hiss' has been chosen deliberately not only for its sound but also for its slightly dark and sinister connotations. Scalan House is, on the one hand, a story of survival against great odds, but it is also a place with a blood-stained history and the massacre at Culloden took place just a few miles away. So what single word is to be used for conveying so many layers of meaning? Obviously I cannot have my burn babbling, and so I tried 'gabbling', which instantly added a touch of foolishness that was completely unacceptable, 'burbling' likewise. My thesaurus has provided me with such words as 'blabbering, blethering, cackling, gaggling, gibbering, gurgling, gushing, jabbering, murmuring, prattling, rattling, spluttering, spouting, sputtering, yabbering, yattering', none of which will do at all. I shall have to keep on trying.

What this list shows, however, is that English has little respect for running water. None of these words are gracious, all are connected somehow with ideas of excessive or awkward sounds, with foolishness at worst, light-heartedness at best and I wonder why this should be so. Italian is much more respectful to water, but perhaps this is because rhyming patterns in Italian are so inherently sonoric and there are so many of them.

The good literary translator has an instinctive grasp of the very different ways in which languages can be handled and the different things that languages can do. The quasi-synonym is a wonderful instrument for the English writer, and good translators can exploit it to best advantage. A good translator will be able to balance what works in one language with what will work in another, and a great translator will ensure that the reader of the translation feels the power of the original in some meaningful way.

Ciaran Carson is an award-winning poet and translator, whose version of Dante's *Inferno* won the Weidenfeld Translation Prize in 2003. It is not hard to see why, especially when compared with other, worthy scholarly versions. When I gave my son a copy of the Carson version to read, he commented that this was a translation that read like a real poem. Compare the way in which the poet-translator renders the opening lines of canto 32, when Dante is descending fearfully into the lowest part of hell and is struggling for words to express the horror of the place with the respectable but dull prose version by Robert Durling. Here is the Italian version:

> S'io avessi le rime aspre e chiocce
> come si converrebbe al tristo buco
> sovra'l qual pontan tutte le altre rocce,
> io premerei di mio concetto il suco
> più pienamente; ma perch'io non l'abbo,
> non sanza tema a dicer mi conduco:
> ché non è impresa da pigliare a gabbo
> descriver fondo a tutto l'universo,
> né da lingua che chiami mamma or babbo.

There is so much going on in these lines – Dante uses harsh-sounding words, striving to express the inexpressible and such is his state of mind that he falls back into childhood. As language fails him, he returns to the point of origin, implying that he needs a different kind of language to speak about this obscene place. Durling renders it matter-of-factly:

> If I had harsh and clucking rhymes such as befit the dreadful hole toward which all other rocks point their weight,
> I would press out the juice from my concept more fully; but because I lack them, not without fear do I bring myself to speak;
> For it is no task to take in jest, that of describing the bottom of the Universe, nor one for a tongue that calls mommy and daddy.

Carson uses a different strategy:

> Had I some wild barbaric rhetoric
> to suit the gloom of this appalling pit
> which takes the weight of stack on stack of rock

> I would extract more meaning from the pith
> of what I saw within; but since I don't.
> with trepidation do I take this path
> of words; for to describe the fundament
> of all the world is no mere bagatelle,
> nor is it depth for baby-babble meant.

Knowing that he cannot reproduce the sound patterns of the Italian, he opts for a different set of sounds, with images like 'the weight of stack on stack on of rock', a line that draws on English poetic tradition, as does the Shakespearean echoing in the last three lines. Talking to Carson about his work, he told me that paramount for him was what a work sounded like, its musicality and its rhythms. To illustrate this point, he sang the first few lines of *Inferno*, using his expertise in traditional Irish music as a way of trying to think himself into Dante's world. Reflecting on Dante exile from Florence, and the bitter internecine feuding that preceded the threats against his life, Carson compared that world with the Belfast of the years following Bloody Sunday. He also suggested that just as Dante gives the dozens of characters imprisoned forever in hell a chance to speak for the last time in their own voices so a translator has to be mindful of all these different styles of speaking that are heard on every level as Dante descends. To render this variety, Carson again drew on his own daily life using the speech patterns of people around him and encoding their rhythms into his version of the Italian mediaeval epic. One reviewer wrote about how 'bits of vulgar burlesque' move with the rough grain of Dante's speech and 'the stabbing beat of the original', which is a very apt assessment of what this particular translator has done.

I have yet to read his versions of French poets and 18th century Irish, but having read the Dante and worked with Carson in our translation workshop, I can say with confidence that they will not only testify to his talents as a poet, but to his willingness to use dictionaries in an unending process of modest, but essential learning. People who sneer at those of us who love our dictionaries are not worth listening to, and so if you have been feeling inadequate because you look words up all the time, do not. Feel proud instead!

First published in *ITI Bulletin* September–October 2006.

Chapter 9
Translation or Adaptation?

I have been writing about Ted Hughes (1999), the late Poet Laureate for the past few months. He is a writer I admire greatly, not only for his poetry about nature and the Yorkshire landscape of his childhood that shaped his way of seeing the world, but also for his magnificent translations. His *Tales from Ovid*, a translation of Ovid's *Metamorphoses*, was so successful that it went into the best-seller lists when it came out in 1997, not long before his death in 1998. That fact alone says something; not every day does a translation from classical Rome sell hundreds of copies in high-street bookshops.

But it was not enough to deter someone telling me after a recent guest lecture when I was discussing Hughes' translations, that he was 'not really a translator at all'. I asked why not, and was told that he did not translate, he adapted or produced versions of texts, and that was not real translation.

This argument is very difficult to win. Debates about when a translation stops being a translation and becomes an adaptation have rumbled on for decades, but I have yet to meet anyone who can give me an adequate definition of the difference between the two. The basis of the distinction seems to be the degree to which a text that has been rendered into another language diverges from the source: if it seems so close as to be recognisable, then it can be classified as a translation, but if it starts to move away from that source, then it has to be deemed an adaptation. The problem is, though, how close do you have to be, and how far away do you have to move before the labels change?

I have always had problems with this distinction. I do not have problems with writers who make it very plain that they have used the source as a starting point and signal that in their versions. Ezra Pound used the term 'homage', in his *Homage to Sextus Propertius* thereby signalling very plainly that he had used the Latin as his inspiration. When a pedantic scholar complained that he had been unfaithful, he rebutted the accusation by stating bluntly that he had never intended to produce a translation. More recently, in 2004, Josephine Balmer (2004a, 2004b) brought out two books combining translations and her own poetry in innovative ways, both using Catullus as her starting point, with very significant titles – *Chasing Catullus* and *Poems of Love and Hate,* where the names of the authors are given jointly as Catullus and Josephine Balmer. The publicity blurb notes that here we are in 'border territory, the no-man's land between poetry and translation'. This is an odd way of putting it. For surely what Balmer is doing is exercising her own creativity while engaging with the creative work of another writer. Hardly no-man's land!

Some writers use phrases such as 'based on', or 'from the work by x' or 'adapted from', but when a writer claims that he or she has produced a translation, then I believe that is how we should see it. Balmer claims to translate; in my view, that is exactly what she does, regardless of how close to the actual words of a source she may be. As translations can never be the same as the original, they cannot ever be so faithful that nothing changes in the transfer process; it simply is not possible to do this. Languages are different. The skilful translator therefore finds ways of reshaping the source for a new set of readers. That is what the job of translating is. In some cases, as with Catullus, there is so much doubt about the originals that the translator has to exercise judgement and make conscious choices. Balmer cites the case of one scholar who said that he had changed his mind about what the original was actually saying so many times that he no longer had any clear position at all. Moreover, some 'originals' may themselves be translations. One of Catullus' poems is actually a translation from the Greek of Sappho, and in contemplating translating this, Balmer reflects on whether an English reader should in some way, consciously or unconsciously, be made aware of the fact that 'the text they are presented with is a third-hand version'. And if Catullus' Poem 51 is a translation from the Greek, what does that make it in English – a translation of a translation, an adaptation, a metatranslation or some other hybrid form?

The translation or adaptation argument seems to be focussed always around literary texts. When you are translating a legal document, for example, nobody is going to complain that you have produced an adaptation if the two texts are clearly different; the client will acknowledge that you have rewritten the document in accordance with the style and the conventions of the culture of the readers for whom it is intended. Any beginner learning about letter-writing conventions will quickly discover that the blunt English 'Yours sincerely' needs to be dressed up in a different kind of rhetoric when the letter is translated into French or Italian.

Yet, nobody complains about a letter being adapted, rather it is accepted that this is a necessary adjustment. So why are we so obsessive when it comes to literary works, what is it that fuels the debate and leads intelligent people to hunker down in trenches, refusing even to contemplate that there can be degrees of freedom for all translators?

Part of the answer may lie in the misconceived ideas about translation that still abound, for translation is not a simple process of linguistic transfer. It is a two-stage activity, that involves careful reading at stage one and skilful writing at stage two. When we are given a translation, what we have is one person's reading of the original text. Twenty different translators will produce twenty different versions, even if those differences are slight, for 20 different readings and endeavours to write up those readings are involved. The interpretation a translator gives to his or her reading of the original will then be reflected in the final product. Moreover, that final product will effectively be a rewriting of the original, as André Lefevere (1992a) has so helpfully argued. Thinking of translation as rewriting helps us to move on beyond the silly idea that a translation must somehow be the same as the original. It can never be the same, for the translator's input combined with linguistic and cultural differences ensure that. The idea of rewriting also helps us to avoid the translation/adaptation distinction: once we accept that what happens when a text is moved from one language to another is that it is rewritten, then trying to set boundaries between translating and adapting ceases to be relevant.

Language teaching has a lot to answer for regarding misconceived ideas about translation, for often translating is seen as a mechanism for testing knowledge of another language by 'reproducing' a text, making it as close to the source as possible. Good translators move on beyond this kind of exercise and bring their own creativity into the equation. So when Ted Hughes translated Euripides' *Alcestis* to be performed by the Northern Broadsides company who specialised in playing classical texts in northern English speech, what he created was a superb, contemporary version of the Greek play. He had often commented on how Yorkshire speech patterns could be traced back to Middle English in an unbroken line of heritage. Now, translating Euripides, he made a play that could be performed by modern vernacular actors, reshaping the conventions and the language to suit modern audience expectations and at the same time creating a work that had roots in an ancient English literary tradition. It is hard to see how this kind of work cannot be considered a translation.

In the 1960s, Ted Hughes and Daniel Weissbort started a journal, *Modern Poetry in Translation*. This journal enabled a great host of poets from around the world to reach an English readership. It is still a valuable resource and a pleasure to read, and what I particularly enjoy are the brief comments by translators about their work. A recent issue has some wonderful translations of poems by Anna Akhmatova, and significantly two of the translators admit to having no Russian. Colette Bryce (2005) makes a very important point: for her, making successful versions of poems depends on 'achieving the tension and the music anew, as these are the untranslatable elements'. She explains how she works as a translator, stressing the relationship that develops, explaining that she 'inhabits' the poems during the writing process. The result is an amalgam of the original and the creative solutions employed by the translator, with the objective of producing a poem that is equally memorable as the one in the source language.

It really is time we stopped quibbling about where translation ends and adaptation begins. A good translation will read like an original, will surprise, move or entertain us, perhaps in different ways from the original, perhaps in similar ways, but it will always be a rewriting of something written somewhere else, in another culture and another time. And since the degree of rewriting will be the responsibility of the translator, we should learn to trust translators more and recognise the value of what they do.

First published in *ITI Bulletin* September–October 2005.

Chapter 10
Translating Style

I recently read the Oxford edition of Tolstoy's *War and Peace*, translated by Louise and Aylmer Maude. To my shame, I had never read it before, and so I was surprised to find myself reading a novel that seemed somehow familiar, resonant with echoes of Jane Austen. This was an unexpected discovery, for generally Jane Austen is compared unfavourably with Tolstoy as someone who writes only about limited domestic milieux rather than broad historical panoramas. Nevertheless, what struck me about the Tolstoy I was reading were Austenesque details of domestic relationships couched in Austenesque language. The question of course is whether this stylistic feature is present in Tolstoy in Russian, or whether it has been introduced through the translators. A second question, to which I shall probably never find an answer is how could I ever discover what was or was not added during the translation process?

We have to trust translators. They undertake to transpose texts written in a language that we do not know and bring them into a language that we can read easily. We all like to talk as though we had direct access to other literatures, so that when I say I have just read *War and Peace*, everyone understands me to be saying I have read Tolstoy. But of course I have not read Tolstoy, because I have no Russian. I have read a translation. I have read the Tolstoy created by a translator, and the echoes of Jane Austen I discerned in my English Tolstoy were put there, consciously or unconsciously, by that translator.

Let us take a step back from the discussion on any specific text, and make sure we are in agreement about what a translation is. For me, the first point to establish with a translation is that it is a text that exists in relation to another text. There is always a starting point, which we can call an original, a source or whatever. If there were not, a translation would not be a translation at all; instead it would be yet another original. In addition, it is important to agree that translation is a complex activity that involves far more than merely transposing words with the help of a dictionary. In the introduction to their book, *Translation and Power*, Maria Tymoczko and Edwin Gentzler (2002: xxi) sum up neatly the complexities of the translation process: 'Translation is not simply an act of faithful reproduction but, rather, a deliberate and conscious act of selection, assemblage, structuration and fabrication – and even, in some cases of falsification, refusal of information, counterfeiting, and the creation of secret codes.'

Translation as a literary practice involves forms of authorship, it involves the translator in decision-making and of course it also involves the translator in rewriting. An example from my own translation practice will help to illustrate this point. The first two lines of a small poem by the Argentinian writer, Alejandra Pizarnik, titled 'Fiesta' posed a particular translation problem that led me to translate a lot more of her writing, because solving it proved very enticing. The problem concerns equivalence, not only word-for-word equivalence, but equivalence in terms of style and poetic effect. Pizarnik wrote:

> *He desplegado mi orfandad*
> *Sobre la mesa, como un mapa.* (Bassnett with Pizarnik, 2000)

Literally translated, this would be:

> I laid out my state of being an orphan
> Across the table, like a map.

I made two changes to this literal version. First, I used the slightly obscure verb 'to unfurl', in order to convey a sense of the movement of unrolling the map. Second, I opted for 'homelessness' to render *orfandad*. I could have gone for a word like 'orphanhood', but that seemed so extreme that readers might pause to wonder whether it really was a word at all and so lose the significance of what for Pizarnik was one of the many keywords that she used throughout her oeuvre. I chose 'homelessness', in the end, because it conveyed a sense of not belonging, albeit one that did not have the connotations of abandonment in childhood. I also felt that 'homelessness' is a powerful word in English (the word 'home' is synonymous with 'house') because it has both a physical and an emotional meaning. Maintaining the shape of her poems in English was important: she always wrote poems that were small and occupied a neat little space on the printed page.

We would probably all agree that translation is a process during which a metamorphosis occurs. A piece of writing that exists in one language is transformed into something else. The original readers disappear and are replaced by a new set of readers, dwelling in another place and in another time. When they read, they will read differently, for the context of reading also changes meaning. One Easter, a service was held in Iraq for British troops, and one of the hymns they sang was the old Victorian favourite: 'There is a green hill far away'. Written by Mrs C.F. Alexander (1823–1895), the hymn is about Christ's crucifixion:

> There is a green hill far away
> Without a city wall
> Where our dear Lord was crucified
> Who died to save us all.

The hymn draws upon the same imagery used by William Blake, in 'Jerusalem', where 'England's mountains green' are equated with the Holy Land in a kind of mystical transformation. But in 2003, in Iraq, that image acquired a different meaning: it was 'translated', delivering not so much a mystical message as one of nostalgia for the distant homeland. This same process must have happened countless times in other contexts, when an image of idealised English greenness reminded singers of home. As Umberto Eco (2001) points out, translation is primarily concerned not with denotation but with connotation, and the connotations words acquire in different contexts are crucial to translations.

Some years ago I published a translation of a poem by Elizabeth Weston otherwise known as Westonia (1582–1610) the English Humanist poet who spent her life in Prague and wrote in Latin. The poem, 'Concerning the flooding of Prague after constant rains', was published in an anthology of poetry of the environment, something that author could never have imagined. The translator's dilemma this time was whether it was ethically justifiable to take a single poem out of the volume in which it had first appeared and place it in a collection with a very contemporary theme. I justified doing this by judging that had Westonia been alive today, she would, on the basis of the subject matter of her poems and what is known of her life story, have probably been politically active and concerned about the state of the planet. I also considered that since her work had languished unread since the last edition of her *Parthenicon* appeared in the middle of the 18th century, it was time she was rediscovered by a new set of readers.

There is now a splendid edition of Westonia's work in English. However, the book is intended for a scholarly readership, and so the translations, though technically accurate, are not poetic. A comparison of the final lines shows the very different strategies employed by the translators. In my version, rhythm is important:

> A boat ploughs through the square, a fish defiles God's shrine;
> runaway waters lap the altar steps.
> Dazed crowds stand by, their garments streaming wet,
> they grieve to see the wreck of all they own.
> Such a sight it was to see the Molda rage;
> so like the flood that Deucalion knew.
> Oh Jove, who tames wild monsters of the deep,
> incline your head and drown these many woes. (Weston, 1991: 48)

The classical references are merged with the horrors of the flood, which has swept through churches and destroyed homes and lives. In the scholarly version, a footnote explains that the reference to Deucalion and the flood appears in Ovid's *Metamorphoses*. The poem is translated literally:

> A skiff ploughs the main square; a fish defiles the shrines of the gods;
> the altar drips with receding floods.
> The crowds stand astonished
> but with soaked clothing,
> and grieve at the total loss to these strange woes.
> Such was their expression, viewing angry Moldau;
> the waves were like those of Deucalion.
> Jehovah, you can tame the sea's monsters and their mad furies;
> submerge all these woes with your nod. (Weston, 2000)

Strictly speaking, the second version is more accurate in terms of linguistic equivalence, but my version has focused on stylistic questions. I wanted to produce something that would be recognisable as a poem today, even though all the rhetorical, formal and referential skills that Westonia employed could not be translated. She was a mistress of Latin verse forms, regarded as one of Europe's finest Latin poets during her brief lifetime. My version, inadequate though it may be in some respects, tries to give contemporary readers some sense of her poetic ability.

Willis Barnstone (1993) has produced a witty 'ABC of Translating Poetry', which has some great advice for translators. The translator of poetry, he insists, must be a poet. The critical moment for a poem is when it changes languages, and it is the responsibility of the translator to ensure that its poetic quality comes across. The translator (who he refers to as the translator-poet) must always use contemporary language and avoid archaisms: 'Old writers will not lose the centuries of their age when heard in modern diction' (Barnstone, 1993). This is sound advice, as is his comment that the skill of the translator-poet is tested by strictures. Sometimes, by staying too close to the original, all that results is a literal, dull poem. Nevertheless, the problem is that the strictures imposed by the original can never be forgotten.

Barnstone offers a beautiful image about the paradox of struggling to be creative while working within the parameters set by the original writer: 'The Chinese call the method of the great Tang poets of working imaginatively while being bound by strictures, "dancing in chains".'

The idea of dancing in chains is an apt one when we consider the difficulties of translating the individual style of a writer. Sometimes, translation cannot succeed because there is no adequate framework in the target language, no equivalent stylistic tradition. This is the case with Jane Austen in Italian, where despite the best efforts of translators her work has never acquired the popularity of Emily Brontë, for example, because Austen's special ironic discourse, so beloved of English readers, does not map onto Italian reader expectations. The impact on Jane Austen of 18th century wit and irony in fiction and essay writing in the English tradition, combined with her natural talent to make her one of the greatest novelists in English. In Italian, she comes across as a minor lady novelist, producing small-scale novels with Mills and Boonish plots.

Yet, sometimes a translator manages the impossible, and introduces a new style, a new form, a new literary language. This is what happened to Chinese poetry in English, after the publication of Ezra Pound's *Cathay* in 1915. Pound was a landmark translator, who translated from many languages, both ancient and modern, but was (and remains) very controversial. He produced his Cathay poems from literal translations by Ernest Fenellosa and a Japanese scholar, Kainan Mori. Pound was therefore working at second hand, unlike his translations from Italian or Latin or Provençal, where he knew the languages well enough to translate without an intermediary. He has often been criticised for inadequate knowledge of Chinese or Japanese, and for deliberately altering the source text for his own ends. Where I would defend Pound (1963) is that whenever he altered the original, the result was beautiful. He was motivated by stylistic concerns, by a desire to write aesthetically pleasing translations for English readers, and he succeeded. His translations set a benchmark for translation from Chinese, generating what can be termed an entire English discourse of Chineseness. George Steiner (1992: 377) describes some of the poems in Pound's *Cathay* as 'masterpieces', which have 'altered the feel of the language and set the pattern of cadence for modern verse'. Steiner approves of T.S. Eliot's (1987) descriptions of Pound's Chinese translations as 'translucencies' and argues that the success of his poems is part of a general phenomenon of trust on the part of English readers, who accepted that both Pound's translations and Arthur Whaley's were written in a language that confirmed all the expectations of Western readers. In other words, the idea of what Chinese poetry ought to sound like was already present in the minds of readers, and Pound more than fulfilled those expectations.

Pound himself tried hard to write about how English and Chinese consciousness differ. He suggested, for example, that when asked to define something, a European would move increasingly towards abstraction. Asked to define 'red', the European would resort to scientific explanation of colour, whereas the Chinese would go back to the ideogrammatic form. Hence, 'red' would become an abbreviated picture of all things red – flamingo, rose, iron rust and cherry. Pound's argument was that two different processes were at work that he could identify, but that the Chinese language, as Fenellosa had argued 'had to stay poetic; simply couldn't help being and staying poetic in a way that a column of English type might well not stay poetic' (Pound, 1960: 22).

What Pound managed to do was to introduce a new style of poetry into English, by showing readers a new way of looking and hence of reading. That he succeeded is not in doubt; the *haiku* has become an accepted literary form in many languages, and Pound's stylistic experiments opened the way for many other writers. He successfully encouraged readers to tackle unfamiliar works, produced in unfamiliar languages that broke conventional expectations of poetic for. Octavio Paz, the Mexican writer and translator, has said that he believes Pound virtually began modern poetry in English, through his translations, which introduced an imagistic style of writing into English.

Pound was more aware than many writers of the important role translation can play in introducing innovation into literatures, but he was also fully aware of the limitations of translation. His forthright opinions were controversial: he claimed, for example, that Gavin Douglas's translations of Virgil were better than the Latin originals, but complained that he had no idea where English readers could get an idea of ancient Greek 'since there are no satisfactory translations' (Pound, 1960: 58). The poet Charles Tomlinson (1982) took up Pound's remarks about Gavin Douglas, and suggested that when a translation is so successful that it actually enters into the target literature, this is because a metamorphosis has taken place and something from the past that was in some mysterious way recoverable is transformed into a meaningful present. Tomlinson points out that

Douglas's translation of the *Aeneid* was completed in 1513, the year of the devastating defeat of the Scottish armies at Flodden Field. Readers living in that age of instability and disorder responded to the powerful, deeply moving imagery of Pound's own Chinese translations. Crucial to the success of such translations is the translator's ability to re-imagine a work written in a distant place for readers struggling to come to terms with what is happening in their own world.

Yet, ultimately, though we may analyse ways in which texts are manipulated through translation and consider the many cultural and ideological factors that pertain in any act of translating, it is important never to lose sight of the translator, working often in isolation, struggling with the constraints of what may be a restrictive literary system or with the demands of a market that limits choice and curtails innovation. We need to trust translators, to respect them and to recognise the vital role they play in regenerating literature by introducing new forms, new styles of writing and new ways of seeing.

First published in *The Linguist* 43 (1), 2004.

Chapter 11
Telling Tales

Although I have spent years teaching literature and translation, I still cannot work out why the translator and the writer should be seen as two separate entities in our culture. After all, translators of literature have to be able to write well in order to satisfy their readers, and it seems strange to deny them the title of 'writer' when they are effectively the (re)writers of work by other authors. The current critical success of the Turkish author Orhan Pamuk is due, in part, to his own literary talents, but it is also due to the literary talent of his English translator, Maureen Freely, an acclaimed novelist in her own right. When judges of literary prizes consider whether to select Pamuk's work for an award, what they are actually considering is Freely's version of Pamuk. She is his English-language writer. Similarly, all those English writers who claim to have been inspired by Russian novels are actually talking about the translations they have read. I have no idea what Tolstoy is like in Russian; my access to his work is entirely through his translators, principally Constance Garnett.

In 2006, Peter Bush and I co-edited a collection of essays by well-known translators, all of whom were invited to discuss their working experiences as writers. Titled *The Translator as Writer*, the book seeks to explore how literary translators work and how they see themselves in relation to the writers they have chosen to translate. Some translate living writers, with whom they can establish a working relationship; others translate writers who have been long dead, often canonical figures who have been translated many times before. However, the task for the translator remains the same: to bring the work of a writer to a new reading public, and to try to ensure that the pleasure of reading is reproduced effectively in the second language.

One major reason for writing the book was to explore whether there are any valid distinctions between the role of the writer and that of the translator. What emerged is that the boundary between different kinds of writing is very fuzzy indeed, and the creativity required of a literary translator is no less than that required of a monolingual writer. What differs is the way in which translators and writers approach their task at the outset: the task of translation inevitably involves a preliminary stage of closely reading a work written by somebody else. Anthea Bell points out that whatever theories a writer or translator may hold there is little – if any – discernible difference between the end products of either. Josephine Balmer goes further, declaring that 'the one leads into the other and in their continued practice, the two become indivisible' (Balmer, 2006: 184–195).

This indivisibility between writing and translating is apparent once we start to consider the careers of many great literary figures who are primarily remembered for their novels, plays or poems, but who also translated. Alexander Pope may be seen as a great satirist, but in his own time he was hailed as one of the leading translators of Homer. In marginalising the importance of translation as a shaping force in literary history, critics have overlooked the significance of the translations made by eminent writers. Who now remembers that George Eliot was a distinguished German translator and translated a number of important philosophical works, including Spinoza's *Ethics*? Indeed, the 19th century fascination with German writing led several prominent figures to translate important works, including Samuel Taylor Coleridge, Thomas Carlyle and Matthew Arnold. Sir Walter Scott translated Goethe's earliest play, *Götz von Berlichingen mit der eisernen Hand*. Poetry, plays, novels and philosophical and political treatises all found their way into English, with Carlyle playing a leading role in coordinating their translation. Yet, when we think about the Age of Romanticism, we do not immediately think of the importance of translation, nor do we reflect upon how much time and energy writers were expending on it.

There are two basic questions that need to be addressed: why did so many writers choose to translate? And why were their translations so often overlooked? Both questions are, I believe, connected. There has been resistance to the idea that translation is a major force for innovation in literary history, since this does not always fit comfortably with nationalistic theories of creativity, which tend to highlight the importance of 'native' products, and play down the importance of imported forms and ideas. But writers have always gone into the wider world in search of inspiration, and when they have found works that they admire they have tried out their literary skills by endeavouring to reproduce those works in another language. D.H. Lawrence so admired Giovanni Verga that he translated many of the great Italian's novels and short stories, including *Cavalleria Rusticana*. He translated Verga almost obsessively, and undoubtedly Verga's *verismo* style had an impact on his own writing. What is less well known, however, is that Lawrence also co-translated a work by the Russian writer Ivan Bunin.

When a writer takes the time to translate something written by another author he or she always has a good reason, whether it is to experiment with alternative modes of writing, push the boundaries of their own style, or simply because they wish they could have written it in the first instance. In other words, translating a certain work is often a logical next step in one's development of becoming a writer.

Poets such as Shelley, Byron, Swinburne and Rupert Brooke have translated from various languages, both ancient and modern. In some cases they learned these languages at school, but others acquired languages through travel and, more often, through reading extensively. It was not uncommon for an educated man or woman in the 19th century to read competently in several ancient and modern languages. In some cases, family history played a role in language learning, as with the Rossettis.

Dante Gabriel Rossetti's translations of early Italian poetry are qualitatively far better than his poetic ballads written in English. Another Pre-Raphaelite, William Morris was also a prolific translator, from Old French, Latin, Greek and Icelandic, to name but four, and his Icelandic saga translations fed directly into his later prose writing. He discovered the sagas while travelling in Iceland, and also wrote an account of his journey. The hugely successful 19th-century American poet Henry Wadsworth Longfellow was an extraordinarily successful translator and used his translations as a basis for imitations that appealed to a vast public, such as *Tales of a Wayside Inn*.

Classical literature has always presented a particular challenge to writers. John Keats' ode 'On First Looking into Chapman's Homer' pays tribute to the first really great English version of Homer. At that time, John Dryden and Alexander Pope were already well established as pre-eminent translators of classical works from Latin and Greek. Interestingly, Keats did not have a privileged education and so had no Greek himself, hence his respect for the translation. In contrast, Matthew Arnold engaged in a bitter quarrel with Francis Newman about the correct way to translate ancient works for modern readers, which resulted in his famous essays, 'On Translating Homer', published in 1860, which established a benchmark for the ideal translation. Although Arnold's views on translation are now well known, it may come as a surprise to learn that Elizabeth Barrett Browning also translated from Greek, publishing a version of Aeschylus's *Prometheus Bound* in 1833. Robert Browning also translated several Greek tragedies, and a host of writers, including Gerald Manley Hopkins, Thomas Hardy, W.B. Yeats and A.E. Housman translated occasional speeches or fragments.

In the 20th century, writers such as W.H. Auden, Stephen Spender, Louis MacNeice, C. Day Lewis, T.S. Eliot and Aldous Huxley produced translations. Ezra Pound's astonishing *Cantos* were forged through his translation activity of many years, and he is perhaps the most important writer to have raised interest in Chinese and Japanese literature. Yet, the role of translation in the literary development of these and so many other writers has often been overlooked, perhaps because they themselves did not lay enough emphasis on the importance of translating.

Today, writers tend to be more overt about the importance of translating in their lives. Nobel laureates such as Derek Walcott and Seamus Heaney have produced extraordinarily powerful translations, with Heaney's version of *Beowulf* becoming a best-seller in 1999. The late Poet laureate Ted Hughes also made the list of best-sellers with his translation of sections of *Ovid*, titled *Tales from Ovid*. Hughes was a prolific translator, and the forthcoming study of his translation works by Daniel Weissbort will cause many readers to revise their views on whether translation is a secondary activity to the so-called 'original' writing.

A measure of the interface between writing and translating can be found in the work of such figures as Tony Harrison, Edwin Morgan and Christopher Logue, whose writings are extremely difficult to categorise. All are effectively translator-poets, people whose writing draws upon different sources of inspiration, some of which have already been composed in other languages by other people.

Over the last 30 years or so, literary criticism has undergone a revolution and the concept of canonical literature has been challenged. How do writers become canonised? Who determines and sustains the canon? Why are so many writers outside the canon, particularly if they happen to be women? Clearly, there are some writers whose work has endured despite changes in taste over the centuries, but as we question the formation of literary canons, we need to remember the vital role played by translation in the development of world literatures.

Far from being a marginal activity, translation has played a central role in shaping literature. Choosing to remember only certain works by eminent writers while overlooking the importance of their translation activity skews the picture of their achievements. It is a historical distortion. Let us give the last word to Madame de Staël, who remarked in 1820 that 'the most eminent service one can render to literature is to transport the masterpieces of the human spirit from one language into another' (de Staël in Lefevere, 1992b: 17).

First published in *The Linguist* 45 (4), 2006.

Chapter 12
Pride and Prejudices

Every year in the autumn hundreds of students sign up for degree programmes in British universities, and usually lecturers are seen rushing around meeting and greeting them all and introducing them to their new environment. But this year, most lecturers are preoccupied with other matters, notably the final stages of preparation for the Research Assessment Exercise, known acronymically as the RAE, the peer review of their research that comes round every five or six years or so. Every academic has to submit four pieces of original research that are then judged and given points out of four by a panel, along with all kinds of details about their institutional research culture. This is a complicated, time-consuming exercise, that is taken deadly seriously because there are funding consequences for very high and very low scores, and the final deadline is later this year, so nobody wants to do badly. But the RAE is also highly controversial because the definition of top quality research is by no means clear, and when we come to translation as research, the waters are very muddy indeed.

It has long been the case that the study, and especially the practice of translation has been looked down upon by many academics. When I started my career some 30 years ago, I was advised not to list translations as serious publications and given to understand in no uncertain terms that I would be far more gainfully employed were I to write a 4000 word critical essay on a couple of novels than to actually translate a novel myself. I kept my translations to myself, and for a long time I did not list them on my C.V. I translated poetry, fiction and plays, including a play by Luigi Pirandello for its British premiere, but offered as evidence of my research only the academic books and articles. Bizarrely, what I wrote *about* translation appeared to be more highly regarded than the translations themselves. That attitude has been modified over the years, but only slightly and along with original writing, translation is still relegated to the margins of academic respectability. I have often been advised not to list the work of which I am most proud, in particular my poetry translations and I submit some of my duller academic publications for the panel to scrutinise well aware that they will be taken more seriously as 'research'. I do this in the full knowledge that what I am colluding with is both wrong headed and foolish.

Translation requires all kinds of skills that by anyone's standards imply a high level of both knowledge and ability, and literary translation necessarily involves research. To translate a novel you have to read with immense care, you have to learn a great deal about the novelist, understand the stylistic devices that writer employs, which may well mean reading all his/her other work, strive to render every nuance, ambiguity and allusion, locate the novel in its historical context and then start to render it into another language for a new set of readers in a different time and place. Tomás Eloy Martínez sums the task up nicely when he points out that 'translation is much more than an extremely attentive reading of a text. It also means writing it all over again, recreating it, making it reflect another culture' (Martínez, 2002: 61). The literary critic reads a text, and writes an analysis, whereas the translator reads a text, then rewrites it in another language: why then is the one considered research while the other is considered to be 'just a translation'? This distinction does not make sense.

A friend of mine has just finished a new translation of a major work by a Latin poet that used to be enormously popular but which has more or less disappeared off the cultural radar screen in Europe, and has not been much read for the last two hundred years. The task was therefore doubly difficult – she had to bring back to life a long dead writer and understand, in that process of regeneration, why his writing should have ceased to have popular appeal at a certain moment in time. Without that understanding, it would have been difficult to find the right set of literary and cultural hooks on which to hang the translation. Accordingly, she undertook a vast amount of research into literary history, which shed some light on the way in which tastes had changed during the Age of Enlightenment. Readers today are conditioned by such dramatic shifts of public taste, whether we realise that or not. We need only think of the impact of Romanticism, for example, which altered the way in which people perceived the world around them – landscapes that would, in the 17th century have been regarded as ugly, barbaric and to be avoided became, in the late 18th century, sublime, magnificent and the destination of tourists. Goethe, Byron and Wordsworth did not look with the same eyes as their predecessors, and their writing was accordingly entirely different. So the need to try and understand why a major Latin work should have dropped out of sight was an important stage in learning how best to bring it to readers today. All this preliminary work, in my view, counts as serious research.

My friend also visited some of the places mentioned in the poems, because having a grasp of the topography, the climate and general sense of place can so often be of great help to a translator. Many translators seek to understand the physical environment that underpinned the original work, and sometimes travelling in order to have some sense of that environment can be helpful. Of course it is not necessary, but there are times when it can be helpful, in the same way as it can be helpful for someone writing an analysis of a writer's work. I have just finished a book on Ted Hughes, a poet for whom landscape was extremely important, and I feel sure that my understanding of his writing has been helped by my personal knowledge of Yorkshire.

The undervaluation of literary translation is not confined to the world of universities. It is also very evident in the way in which translations are reviewed. I recently read an excellent review that praised both the original work and the skills of the translator, then noted that the reviewer was the Director of the British Centre for Literary Translation, a solitary voice of correctness, since other reviewers had not bothered to comment on whether the books they were reviewing were translations or not. Some newspapers and journals are better than others in acknowledging whether a book has been translated, but few seem to require reviewers to note the name of the translator as well as that of the original author, and very few bother to mention whether it even is a translation. The standard practice of book reviewers appears to be to treat every work as though it had been written in English in the first instance, ignoring the translator and the translation process.

A number of people working in the field known as Translation Studies have, for some time now, been urging translators to take matters into their own hands and assert their presence more visibly. There are various ways in which this can happen, perhaps most notably for translators to include a short preface to their translations and to negotiate better contracts with publishers that ensure their names are given sufficient prominence. But review editors also have a responsibility, and at a time when internationalisation is a buzz word and everyone is preaching the gospel of cross-cultural communication it is curious that there should still be such reluctance to acknowledge the work of translators in review pages. Eloy Martinez sees translation as vital to the survival of a work, a test of its strength. If a book succeeds in another language, that success is due in large part to the skills of the translator. There have been cases where a relatively humdrum work has become a great success elsewhere because it has been so well translated, just as there are also cases of successful works failing through translation inadequacies, but the point to note here is that the translator is the means by which a work appears in its new linguistic form.

The relegation of literary translation to the margins is outdated and wrong. Monolingual readers need to be helped to understand just how complex translation is and how much research can go into a literary translation. If we could have more public recognition for translators by literary editors, the old prejudices harboured by academics might start to disappear also. There are some faint signs that this is starting to happen, but the process of change is far too slow for an increasingly multilingual world.

First published in *ITI Bulletin* May–June 2008.

Chapter 13
Turning the Page

There was no shouting in the streets at the announcement that from September 2008 the study of set texts by classic European writers in modern language A levels offered by English exam boards was going to end. Pupils will no longer read any 19th-century Russian or French poets and will never have to engage with Thomas Mann or Molière or Carlo Levi. Literature is to be axed, and instead pupils will be required to write a short essay on their own choice of literary subject, whatever that weasel phrase means.

I confess I read this news with sadness even though I know that the study of foreign languages is on the decline and presumably the thinking here is to try and ensure that as many pupils as possible opt to stay with a language, made more 'relevant' by the dropping of works that are considered boring.

The British government's disastrous decision to drop the obligatory study of a foreign language after the age of 14 has already had other serious consequences: the number of pupils who continue with a language to GCSE and beyond has plummeted in the state sector, meaning that serious study of foreign languages is predominantly in the independent schools and that does not chime well with the government's mission to get more pupils from poorer backgrounds into universities. For modern languages this is very serious, because several university departments have been axed and those that survive have a high percentage of students who are not from state schools. Recently, Cambridge announced that as part of its drive to conform to the government widening participation agenda, it would be dropping its traditional foreign language GCSE requirement. The decision to cut literature out of the A-level syllabus is presumably also part of this general school of thought – take languages out of the higher education equation.

What puzzles me is why this should be happening now, why an advanced European nation which has prided itself, especially in recent years on its willingness to take in people from all over the world, a nation where there are schools in which over 40 languages are spoken by the pupils who attend it should be so short-sighted as to cut the next generation off from its European heritage. One answer I have been given more than once is that we in the United Kingdom do not need to learn anybody else's language because the rest of the world is busy learning English. But this answer is entirely unsatisfactory: for a start, British English is now only one of dozens of variants of global English and in any case, you cannot divorce languages from cultures. When you learn a language, you learn about the cultures that use that language, and if English pupils never study anything but English with a bit of conversational French or Spanish on the side, they will have a pitifully inadequate knowledge of how other people in the world think and behave.

Which is, of course, where the study of foreign literatures can be so valuable, for when we read works by great (and not so great) writers, we learn about how people other than ourselves think, behave, feel and act. *War and Peace* and *Pride and Prejudice* are amazing novels because they are peopled with characters full of vitality, who inhabited a Russia and an England contemporaneous with one another that has long since vanished. Reading both novels we can understand more about the great differences between the two cultures, besides admiring the skill of each very different writer, remembering, of course, that most of us are guided to the Russian through the skills of a translator.

Reading other literatures does more than show us aspects of other societies; however, it also shows us different ways of writing and helps us to understand more about the complexities of translation. I can still remember first encountering Paul Verlaine's 'Chanson d'automne', and the pleasure of reading lines like 'les sanglots longs des violins d'automne' in my French A-level class, while realising the impossibility of conveying those patterns of sound into English. You could say that was an early encounter with the problem of literary untranslatability, which I had never heard of at the time; so what I remember is trying in all sorts of ways to render Verlaine's poem and failing dismally along with my fellow pupils. I wonder what the impact of removing literature from the A-level syllabus is going to be on literary translation in a few years time. As one of the judges for the *Times* – Stephen Spender Prize for poetry in translation, I have seen how some teachers encourage their pupils to enter the competition in under-18 category by trying their hand at translating their A-level set texts. Some of the results have been excellent, but must we now suppose that nobody taking a modern language will read any literature in that language unless they go on to study it at university? That seems a depressing prospect.

The other problem I have with diminishing the study of foreign literature, is that it flies in the face of all the evidence of the way in which European literatures are, and always have been, interlinked. All the European literatures have been enriched by translating one another: where would Pushkin have been without Byron, or Baudelaire without Poe, or T.S. Eliot and Seamus Heaney without Dante? I once heard a lecture by a well-known contemporary novelist in which she argued that the English 20th-century novel owed everything to the 19th-century Russian novelists. Literary movements transcend linguistic barriers – what we call the English Romantic writers of the late 18th and early 19th centuries read avidly in several languages, borrowed from one another, exchanged ideas and themes and forms. Byron's masterpiece *Don Juan* took the Italian ottava rima form to new heights, Coleridge read widely in German and even the poet regarded as archetypally English, the bard of the Lake District, William Wordsworth drew inspiration from other languages and, especially, from the period he spent in France.

Writers have never allowed themselves to be constrained by languages or cultures. Matthew Arnold, who had a great deal to say about both poetry and translation, declared famously in a quote that I use over and over again with my students, that no single event or literature is 'adequately comprehended except in relation to other events, to other literatures'. He said that in 1857, and it is just as valid today, probably even more so. In an age when travel was a more difficult, writers, artists and intellectuals reached out beyond their own national limits, either because they were privileged enough to travel or because they wanted to know more about other cultures through reading, whether in translation or by learning another language.

There is another deleterious effect of the move away from foreign language learning in schools in the United Kingdom. Over the last few years there has been a revolution in universities across Europe as a result of what has come to be known as the Bologna Process. This is an agreement, signed by ministers of education from all over the continent to create a European Higher Education Area by 2010 that will enable students to move freely between universities regardless of nationality. For this freedom of movement to happen, there has to be a common university system in place, and since 1999 when the Bologna agreement was signed there has been a huge restructuring of European university systems that has brought chaos at times, but which is undoubtedly helping student mobility. Here in the United Kingdom, however, we have dragged our feet about Bologna, and the result is that while hundreds of thousands of other European students gain experience of living and studying in different countries, only a tiny number of UK students cross the Channel, deterred by the high cost of university education in the United Kingdom and also, significantly, by their lack of language skills.

Access to another culture through another language should not be seen as a privilege or an oddity; it should be considered a fundamental element of any decent education. The young people who take advantage of the opportunity to complete their degrees in more than one country have a great competitive advantage over those who can only function in one language, and will be better equipped as citizens of our increasingly global world. They will not only be able to communicate in more than one language, they will also have some grasp of the history, culture and ethos of somewhere that is not their native land. Taking language learning out of secondary schools was a bad mistake; taking what little literature that remains out of the A-level syllabus can only compound that error.

First published in *ITI Bulletin* May–June 2008.

Chapter 14
Poetry in Motion

Every week or so, stories appear in British newspapers about the parlous state of language learning in schools. Whereas once upon a time studying foreign languages was regarded as necessary, now pupils are able to forget all about language study after the age of 14, and few, if any, begin studying another language before secondary school in any case.

This situation in the schools has a knock-on effect at university level too, and numbers have dropped radically in modern language departments, leading some vice-chancellors to close them down. The government is intending to make the study of foreign languages available to primary school children after 2012, but by then a whole generation will have been lost and given the declining interest in universities, it is questionable as to whether there will be enough trained teachers to put the language strategy into operation at all.

I share the concerns of many of my colleagues about this state of affairs, which seems absurdly shortsighted in an international age and bordering on the xenophobic when we consider our proximity to the rest of Europe. So I was delighted when asked to serve as a judge on a translation competition aimed specifically at young people.

The Stephen Spender Memorial Foundation, in partnership with *The Times*, initiated a poetry prize last year, with one category for under-18s and another for translators aged between 19 and 30. It was hoped that entrants from both schools and colleges would be encourage, and that the competition would send out a positive signal to beleaguered teachers at all levels. No restrictions were put on the length of entries, or on the languages, but all entrants were asked to provide a short commentary, of not more than 300 words, giving some indication of how they had set about the task of translation.

The results exceeded all our expectations. We received over 130 entries, in a huge range of languages, both ancient and modern, European and non-European. The seriousness with which the entrants approached the competition was clear from both the translations themselves and the little commentaries. In some cases, teachers had obviously encouraged their classes to enter, and so variations on the same poem, often a set text for the GCSE or A/S level, were sent in. In other cases, the entrants showed great individuality and creativity, choosing little-known works and experimenting bravely with forms and language. One entrant was only nine years old.

The judges read all the entries anonymously, though we did have the age of all translators before us. Although asked to list first-, second- and third-prize winners in each category, we quickly agreed that we would also have a highly commended category as well; such was the diversity and high quality of many of the entries. Indeed, all the dire stories about the decline of language learning were forgotten once we started reading, and both the number of entrants and the quality and range of the translations paint a much more hopeful picture of what is happening in schools and universities across the country.

Numbers may have gone down, language learning may be seen as less interesting and less desirable than it once was, but there are a lot of young people out there doing very good work indeed, to judge by our competition entries.

We each read all the poems separately, having been provided with both the original and the translation. Where we felt that a poem was good but were unable to read the original, we sought specialist assistance. When we came together to compare notes and to draw up a short list, we were pleased to see the extent to which we had a consensus. Obviously each of us had our favourites, but we came to a shared conclusion with a minimum of disagreement. A principal criterion was, obviously, how well the poem worked in English, how ably the translator had shaped the English language in providing a version of his or her original. Then we looked at the strategies employed by the translators, at how they had succeeded in conveying the force of the original and whether the translation was in any way misleading. By this, we did not mean unfaithful or just plain inaccurate, rather we wanted to be assured that the translator had understood the original and, in making an English version of it, had thought creatively about solving the many problems thrown up by the translation process. One translation in the highly commended section was a version of an Anglo-Saxon poem, *Wulf and Eadwacer*, that eschewed the original form to create a new, modern poem that the judges felt was both innovative and, in its own way, true to the source.

When we looked at our final selections, we were astonished to see that we had selected poems from many different languages. In the under-18 category, the three winners were J.C. Potts' translation of Catullus Poem 63, from the Latin, Adrian Pascu's version of Ion Minulescu's *Dead Man's*

Balla from the Romanian, and Holly Hughes' rendering of Victor Hugo's *Tomorrow at Dawn*. Commended were translations from French and Spanish. In the over-18 category, the three winners were Mark Leech's version of the Anglo-Saxon poem *The Dream of the Rood*, Sasha Dugdale's translation of Elena Shvarts' *Memory's Sideways Glance* from the Russian, joint second prize-winner with Paul Howard, who translated G.G. Belli's Roman dialect *The Good Life* into Yorkshire dialect. The three commended translations were from Chinese, Old Norse and Anglo-Saxon.

The range of ancient and modern languages took us by surprise, as did the very mature use of language in the winning entries and the young translators' awareness of what they were trying to achieve.

The commentaries were particularly fascinating. Most of the translators wrote honestly about the difficulties they had encountered, some offering self-assessments that acknowledged their own shortcomings. My academic interest was aroused by the fact that some of the best commentaries were written by translators working from Latin, Greek and Russian, which made me wonder whether there is more emphasis on grammar and on poetics in the teaching of those languages than in the more conventionally taught modern European languages where the conversational approach prevails. Some schools submitted several entries, testimony of very high-quality teaching and commitment to language learning. Several translators wrote about their passion for a particular writer or a particular poem, and several also said that they were motivated by a desire to make accessible poetry that had previously not been translated into English or was barely known. At the other extreme, a few entrants attempted very well-known poems that have been translated frequently, often by well-established writers. One did not know whether to admire the bravery of such attempts or shake one's head at the foolhardiness of a teenager competing with the likes of Seamus Heaney or Ted Hughes.

'Translation', wrote the winner of the over-18 category, Mark Leech, 'is only ever an interpretation'. He is right, of course, and one hopes that he will go on offering his beautiful interpretations of Latin poetry for years to come. This simple statement is what makes translating poetry so exciting and at the same time so demanding: the translator offers his or her own individual interpretation to the reader, through the medium of a poem recreated in another language, and where there are ambiguities in the source, as there are so often in poetry, that interpretation may be challenged. The judges actually received a letter complaining about linguistic inaccuracies in one of the winning entries, but we rebutted that pedantic point by recalling Ezra Pound's famous put-down of an academic who complained about inaccuracies in his Homage to Sextus Propertius. Pound pointed out that any fool could translate literally using 'a Bohn crib. Price 5 shillings' (Pound in Bassnett, 1980: 83).

In poetry translation, it is necessary to produce a result that is beautiful, readable and true to the original, although the way in which that truth is defined will depend on the interpretation of the translator.

First published in *ITI Bulletin* March–April 2005.

When this essay was written, the poetry translation prize had only just come into being. Since then, it has become a regular annual event, and some of the winning entries have been published to considerable acclaim. Further information about the prize may be obtained from: www.stephen-spender.org

Chapter 15
When Translation Goes Horribly Wrong

Silvio Berlusconi is the colourful right-wing Prime Minister of Italy, who has recently decided to take on the job of foreign minister as well as the post he already holds. His supporters adore him, his many opponents despise him, but Berlusconi prides himself on his cosmopolitanism and his ability to interact with the rest of the world. A major plank in his electoral campaign was the promotion of an image of a modern Italian state, assisted, of course, by the powerful media empire he controls.

It was therefore with some astonishment that Italian readers of *La Repubblica*, the equivalent of *The Independent*, learned that one of Berlusconi's media projects, that is the provision of up-to-date biographies of English members of his cabinet released on the internet had gone horribly wrong. What happened to the three 'I's' of Berlusconi's campaign, the paper asked, the three I's being *Internet*, *Impresa* (business) and *Inglese* (English)? On the internet there were a set of biographies translated into English so awful that only someone with no knowledge of the language whatsoever could have allowed it to go out into the public domain. A few random samples give some idea of the whole. Buttiglione (Ministro delle politiche comunitarie) is described as 'been born to Gallipoli, conjugated, father of four daughters, he lives to Rome where he is ordinary university professor'. Apparently 'he graduated himself under the guide of Prof. the Augusto of the Walnut'. Bonaiuti (Sottosegretario di stato alla Presidenza del Consiglio) seems to have had a journalistic career, since 'from 1975 it is sended special, before I. economia and the finance ... it knows four languages, it has collaborated with the BBC and with other average foreign'. Bonaiuti is duly proclaimed 'megaphone of the President Berlusconi and Italy Force'. 'Italy Force' we are told in the entry for Claudio Scajola, 'is by now one agile efficient instrument, taken root on the territory, respected from allied and opposing, able to choose credible candidates to propose the constituents'.

Berlusconi's women fare no better. Stefania Prestigiacomo (Ministro per le pari opportunità), 'been born to Siracusa ... in 1990, to 23 years, he has been elect Young president of the Group Entrepreneurs of Siracusa' while in 1994 'it has been elect to the Room in the proportional list of Italy Force'. Variously described as she, he and it in the same entry, Prestigiacomo is currently 'elect in the uninominale college of Siracusa', whatever that might mean.

Translation howlers are always going to amuse, and anyone who knows Italian can see where some of the above are coming from. The problem with these documents, however, is that they contain just about every translation howler it is possible to make. There are mistakes in the grammar, syntax, spelling, there are the famous 'false friends', that is, words in one language that look like words in another language but mean something entirely different (congiugato in Italian means 'married'), names are translated when they should not be (Professor Augusto of the Walnut is a literal translation of the respectable name della Noce) while Italy Force is a literal rendering of the name of Berlusconi's party, Forza Italia.

No sooner had *La Repubblica* informed the world with some glee what had happened than the website vanished, to be replaced with an announcement declaring that the document had simply been a rough draft. Doubtless heads rolled somewhere behind closed doors and the individuals responsible for allowing such an incompetent document are now gainfully employed elsewhere, but the fact that it could have appeared in the first place is significant. What it shows is that despite being a multi-millionaire media mogul and international political figure, Berlusconi has no sense of the complex processes that are involved in any act of translating.

The Forza Italia biographies have all the hallmarks of having been produced by a computer programme, and translation by computers is nothing new. But someone has to set up the programme, someone has to monitor it and someone has to take responsibility for the quality of the final produce, which certainly did not happen in this case. For a government that wants to demonstrate its internationalism and its commitment to new technology to make such an elementary mistake is astonishing, but, sadly, it is not unusual. Few people who have not engaged in translation themselves understand the difficulties and the care needed to take something meaningful in one language and render it in another.

Translators, often poorly paid and anonymous, are essential in today's world. What September 11 showed the world was the terrifying complacency of native English speakers who assumed that everyone thought as they did. It also showed how skilfully international terrorist networkers can exploit their knowledge of languages and cultures to blend in invisibly around the world.

Many in the English-speaking world have been stunned to discover the depth of resentment felt by millions whose views have simply never been heard because they were never translated. This is the downside to the spread of global English of course: as more and more people learn English, so fewer English speakers feel any need to learn other languages and rely increasingly on translations, without pausing to consider how flawed those translations might be. A team of experts in Arabic language and culture was rounded up to analyse the Bin Laden videos, as it dawned on the US government that translation is so much more than simply taking a word in one language and substituting a word in another. Different languages reflect different thought processes, different cultural values and different world visions. Good translators know that, and try to negotiate the complex layers of difference that monolinguals do not even know exist. As language learning declines even more rapidly in this country, government needs to act to reverse the trend, because we need more experts in intercultural understanding, not fewer and you do not train good translators without solid language learning programmes.

One question still niggles: the first of the biographies on page 1 was Berlusconi's own, and that one was in perfect, idiomatic English without a single mistake – which made the others look even more ridiculous. Could it be that someone knows more about media manipulation through translation than any of us?

First published in *The Linguist* 41 (2), 2002.

Chapter 16
Living Languages

Taking part in a discussion about bilingualism, I was interested to hear someone state that a good translator should have 'perfect knowledge' of both the language from which and the language into which he or she translates. That phrase, 'perfect knowledge', bothered me. What, after all, is perfect knowledge and can such knowledge ever exist? More to the point, can we ever have anything even approximating to perfect knowledge of one language, let alone two? Never a week goes by that I do not resort to a dictionary to look up some word or phrase that is either used in a way unfamiliar to me or which I have never come across before, and I keep my thesaurus in the kitchen, where I can consult it all the time. A thesaurus is particularly handy for crossword puzzles! Writers and translators need such reference books, precisely because we acknowledge that we do not have a 'perfect' grasp of any language.

The broader question, of course, is how exactly we determine linguistic competence. Here, research into bilingualism is fascinating. Not so many years ago, bilinguals were regarded as having lesser brains than monolinguals, since it was presumed that the presence of two languages in anyone's head diminished the 'perfect knowledge' of both. Some of the early IQ tests in the United States appear to have been designed to show that bilinguals were intellectually inferior to monolinguals, a useful assumption to make when a state is trying to show that immigrants are lower down the social food chain. Thankfully, bilingualism has lost that stigma and these days it is seen as an asset, but we are still unsure about how to define bilingualism with any precision. Should we make a distinction, for example, between people who learn two languages from the outset, and those who have a mother tongue but add another language to a high level of competence later? Is the former, as some scholars have suggested, more of a 'true' bilingual, if such a creature can be said to exist?

My view, born out of personal experience, is that this is a highly complex field that defies categorisation. I have met bilingual speakers, taught two languages from birth, who are demonstrably not competent in either, and I have met people who have added an extra language in adulthood and are as fluently spoken and well informed as any native speaker. And what are we to make of people who, though linguistically competent, are culturally ill informed, given that language can never be divorced from the context in which it is used.

Recently, I was attending a conference in Lisbon when I had a strange linguistic experience. I have a particular relationship with Portuguese; as a child, I spoke it fluently, and moved in and out between Portuguese and English unproblematically. Then we moved to Italy, Portuguese had to be set aside as I attended a crammer to prepare myself for entering Italian school before starting to study in a completely new language. Italian took over as the dominant second language, not least because formal learning of other languages, such as Latin and French, had to be done through Italian. I put my Latin proses into Italian, and transferred Italian paragraphs into Latin. Italian became the bridge language, through which I approached all subsequent languages. To this day, when I speak any other language, be it Spanish or French, it is with an Italian accent, not an English one.

But the relationship with Portuguese was not entirely dead. I continued to read books, and would say that by the time I finished university I was a fluent Portuguese reader, albeit always with a dictionary to hand. In adulthood I started going on holiday with my family to Portugal, re-encountering the spoken language. Here, though I had problems, spoken Portuguese was extremely difficult for me, and try as I might I could not find a way back into the language I had once known so well. I experienced it like you experience rain on a windscreen – you know it is wet and cold and you know that raindrops make a noise, but inside a car you do not actually feel any of that. You sit there, aware of rain but not actually feeling it or hearing it.

After a few years, I became aware that the language was somehow raining directly onto me, wetting me, as it were. I felt closer to it; I was by now managing to speak, though my Portuguese was contaminated by Spanish and marked by an Italian pronunciation. Then the other day came this new stage of awareness. Halfway through a conference session, I suddenly realised that I was able to understand everything that was being said, able to laugh at jokes and pick up on nuances. That evening, in a Fado restaurant, the sensation grew on me that the language had somehow become internalised, it was flowing inside me rather than raining on me from without. I found phrases echoing in my head from childhood and I found myself able to plumb a depth of linguistic knowledge that presumably had been buried somewhere. It was an extraordinary sensation; the language was somehow coming back to life within me, acquiring a deeper meaning and resuscitating memories.

What makes my story curious, though, is that Portuguese had supplanted an even earlier language, one acquired when very tiny, Danish. Here though, since I learned that language before I had any kind of formal schooling, hence before I was able to read or write, nothing remains. I took a course for a year as an undergraduate in hopes of reacquiring some of the lost Danish, but I never did. However, I was once asked to do an interview with an expert on accents, who correctly identified that in my everyday spoken English there are traces of both Italian and Portuguese and even of a Scandinavian language, which shows that the brain processes linguistic material in extraordinary ways and nothing is ever completely lost.

What kind of a bilingual, one may ask, is someone like myself who has always had two languages in her head, though not the same languages throughout her life. No sense of perfect knowledge here, rather a shifting reality. Moreover, as one moves from country to country, the cultural context loses its immediacy and starts to fade. Today, I feel very much at home whenever I go back to Italy, comfortable but a foreigner in Portugal and am no more than an enthusiastic visitor to Denmark. Time and absence have a big impact on language competence, and that which is familiar can lose its meaning as life moves on. A common complaint by bilinguals is that if they stay too long away from the place where one of their languages is spoken, they start to lose ground as the language develops and changes and they stay locked in a time warp. One friend told me he needs to go home every six months because any longer period away means that he starts to feel a sense of distancing beginning to materialise.

Of course not everyone has the luxury of doing this. Exiles, refugees, emigrants often leave their homeland forever, and keep their languages alive through memory and interaction with others who find themselves similarly displaced. Can they still be said, as the years pass, to be bilingual? I think they can. What my experience has shown me is that while it is impossible to define bilingualism and impossible certainly to talk about there being perfect levels of knowledge, the ways in which the brain processes language are very complex indeed. Being exposed to more than one language from the outset may not necessarily result in a child growing up to be expert in two languages, but it will certainly open up possibilities for linguistic variety and possibly also for later language acquisition. It is notable that many translators of my acquaintance have interesting and varied linguistic stories to tell, about languages they spoke and lost, about growing up in different countries and about parents speaking to them in more than one language. Translators often have fascinating personal histories where their languages are concerned, and though there are some who acquire a second language at university or later, many have encountered other languages from an early age. In short, it seems that many translators choose that profession because they have an engagement with different languages that they probably could not begin to explain. It is that engagement that leads to open-mindedness and to a willingness to acknowledge that we all need dictionaries because our knowledge cannot ever be perfect. Recognising the impossibility of perfection is what, in my view, makes a good translator.

First published in *ITI Bulletin* January–February 2006.

Chapter 17
All in the Mind

Some time ago, in the *ITI Bulletin*, I wrote about the curious experience of rediscovering the Portuguese of my childhood. That language which had once been so familiar had faded, obscured by the Italian that took over as my principle language from the age of 11 and then by the other languages I learned later. I could always read Portuguese comfortably, but I could no longer speak it and had some difficulty understanding native speakers as well. But over time, a combination of family holidays in Portugal and frequent academic engagements brought the spoken language back into focus and these days I feel comfortable with Portuguese once again.

Recently, I have been thinking a lot about the resurgence in one's consciousness of languages that appeared to have been forgotten. I do not know what terminology to use when embarking on this topic – is it rediscovery or recovery when a language starts to re-emerge in some way from the unconscious – or should it be the subconscious mind? All I know is that what happened a while ago with Portuguese is happening to me with another language of very earliest childhood, Danish.

I learned Danish when very tiny, before I could write, so have nothing but the sounds in my head. When I was at university I enrolled on a one-year course to try and relearn Danish. I managed to read some short stories and some poetry, but my spoken Danish was dreadful and the tutor told me I now had a strong Italian accent. The Danish experiment was not continued, indeed Danish sank below Swedish, another language of family holidays and good friends and regular visits. Not that my spoken Swedish was much better than my Danish; one of my friends almost fell out of the car laughing when I played him my teach yourself spoken Swedish CD and repeated ludicrous sentences in what he said was an accent not heard since the cinema of the 1930s.

The point about these reminiscences, however, is that over the last 12 months or so, long buried languages are coming back to me. I have never rated my German as particularly strong, but recently in Berlin I chatted away to a local taxi-driver about all kinds of things and only when getting out of the cab did I realise that I had been perfectly at home in German, and dialectal German at that.

I am starting to wonder whether this curious process of language resurgence is connected to growing older. I have turned 60, and now have more of the occasional embarrassing senior moments when I forget my partner's phone number or the title of the book I was reading yesterday or the one thing I went out to buy before the shop closed. My mother is 90, and her short-term memory fails her all the time now, but her long-term memory is fantastic. She can remember names, incidents, dates and times from 40, 50 and 70 years ago with clarity and feeling. This is common in older people; it is as though the past begins to intrude on the present and in some way becomes almost more significant.

If memories can rise up that take one back to early childhood, it seems probable that languages can begin to find their way back into the light as well. After all, I spoke Danish fluently until we moved to Portugal, and spoke Portuguese fluently until we went to Italy, and so those languages that were once a part of my daily life must surely still be lodged somewhere in the brain. In Italy, at school I began to learn languages formally, moving from Latin and French on to German. Spanish happened as a kind of accident, it became more and more familiar through films and books, probably because of the other Romance languages I knew, and when I finally took a graduate course in the United States I was fairly competent in that language.

It is not just that I find myself able to understand more in a variety of different languages; I am also dreaming in several languages, and I know that because I can remember precise phrases and conversations when I wake up.

It is all very strange. At a point in life where I was starting to deplore the lack of practice in various languages I had acquired to a greater or lesser degree, I find myself increasingly multilingual unexpectedly. In Denmark, for a PhD viva earlier this year, I translated notices and newspapers for my partner without much effort, then wondered how I came to be able to do that after such a long time without using the language. I seem to be able to understand far better in several languages than I ever thought I could. Somehow, memories of those languages are coming back, and I am starting to wonder whether this is a common experience for others who find themselves, like me, with traces of various languages inside their heads. I would dearly love to hear from any readers who are having similar experiences or from anyone who knows whether any research has been done into this phenomenon.

In parallel with this unexpected but very welcome unblocking of linguistic memories, I find myself more and more drawn to writers who have had to negotiate language changes. Vesna Goldsworthy's (2009) lovely memoir, *Chernobyl Strawberries* explores the ways in which she has come to negotiate two languages, the Serbian of her early life and the English that she refers to at one point as both much more and much less than her mother tongue. Writing about the period when she was working for the BBC World service, she struggles to express the split existence that she is living linguistically:

> I have written millions of words, made love thousands of times, been ill, dreamed and prayed in English. I have cooked countless meals using herbs and spices whose names do not exist in any other language in my mind, while broadcasting in what itself must be becoming something quaintly archaic, the 'RP' spoken by Belgrade's educated classes, the language which, in its own turn, both is and isn't my tongue.

For Vesna Goldsworthy is one of that growing number of gifted international writers who chooses to write in an adopted language, in her case the English that she shares with her husband and his family, and her book explores the ways in which she occupies different linguistic worlds. And like other writers who have had similar experiences of shifting cultures, of losing or rediscovering languages, she also stresses the physicality of language, the sounds and the gestures that accompany words.

Those who move between languages experience those different languages physically in different ways. Sounds resonate in different parts of the body – the lower abdomen, the chest, the throat and the head. I always feel that the more comfortable and grounded I am in a language, the lower in my body do I speak it from. In contrast, if I am less confident, then that language will be spoken from higher up, from the throat or the head. In short, language is also physical and how we speak reflects this.

Experiences of the physicality of language is evident in a collection of essays about language and bilingualism edited by Isabelle de Courtivron (2003): Ariel Dorfman chooses bigamy as a metaphor for bilingualism, Sylvia Molloy writes about 'not quite being there', Ilan Stavans uses the metaphor of a love affair, Leila Sebhar writes about a 'silenced father tongue'. In her essay, which she says is a kind of postscript to her marvellous book, *Lost in Translation*, Eva Hoffman (2003/1989) explores the fear that the loss of a language can evoke. 'When is it safe,' she asks, 'to return to something you have loved and lost?' She tells the story of a Russian poet who had been taken to Israel as a child, having spent some time in a German refugee camp. Growing up, he found that he could remember his German well, but his Russian had disappeared:

> 'I killed it', he said. 'I almost remember the decision to do it- to murder Russian within me.'

Eva Hoffman's (2003/1989) explanation for this is that holding on to the Russian, however beloved it had been as a first language, would have posed a threat to his hopes of becoming a good writer in Hebrew. She herself acknowledges that though she did not seek to kill her Polish, she remembers 'the almost palpable act of pushing it down into some cellar, or coffers, or dark place'.

I find myself wondering whether the Israeli poet found his Russian coming back to haunt him in his later years, as I am finding my earliest languages coming back to me in some way. For language is also intimately linked to identity, and though we can make linguistic choices in adulthood, we have no choice when learning a language in early childhood. I have started to wonder whether my experience of losing Danish and then Portuguese was linked to the trauma of moving homes. I have huge gaps in my memory from my early years, for example, no memories at all of starting school which seems to be strongly imprinted on most people I know, no memories of leaving Denmark at all.

Eva Hoffman (2003/1989) suggests that just as there is cognitive memory, and so there is also cognitive forgetting. She relates how her Polish started to return, started to rush back in some way as though released, and how this happened once she began to feel more confident about how her two languages could live harmoniously within her consciousness, neither one threatening the other.

I am not in a position yet to write with any authority about what is happening to me, or why, and may never fully understand it, but something strange is certainly going on. It is also, in a mysterious way, rather wonderful.

First published in *ITI Bulletin* September–October 2009.

Chapter 18
More than Words

My youngest children are learning Italian, and it is proving a very happy experience for them both. They have grown up with the language swirling around them, and can understand quite a lot, but until now they have never followed a formal course which has taught them a great deal about basic grammar as well as proving highly entertaining. I have always been suspicious of the conversation only method, having learned one of my languages that way, only to forget almost everything because I had no structural frame on which to pin my knowledge. However, setting aside my prejudices for a moment, what has really caught their imagination on this course has been the work they have done on hand gestures.

We often forget that learning a language involves so much more than words, even though we may talk vaguely about 'body language'. Different cultures have different physical modes of expression, from the way they greet one another to the closeness with which they may stand or sit next to one another. The ease with which Indian men hold hands with one another in the street is surprising at first sight to Europeans, as is the way in South India in particular people can uses their neck muscles to move their heads gently from side to side, something I have never managed to master. A handshake is a gesture of politeness in some contexts, but is an intrusion into one's personal space in another. The Japanese system of bowing is impenetrable to foreigners, and we all get it wrong at first if we decide to give bowing a go when in Japan. There is absolutely no universal system of greeting, just as there is no universal system for saying yes or no – in some cases yes is signified by a nod, in others by a shake of the head, a gesture that signifies no right across northern Europe and the Americas. A translator faced with the phrase in a novel 'he nodded assent' would have to alter the gesture or risk confusing a reader when translating into a language where the system of assent entails a shake of the head.

There are all kinds of books for sale at airports that offer advice on intercultural behaviour, warning what you should or should not do when you travel if you want to make a good impression. Some of these contain helpful hints, like not giving your hostess flowers wrapped in paper when in Germany, or not turning up with a chrysanthemum plant in Southern Europe, where such flowers are associated with cemeteries, but I am amazed by how wrong some of these instant intercultural success guides can be sometimes. People who rely on them slavishly can actually create problems where none exist. Not long ago I was hosting a dinner at my university and was sent half a page of instructions on how to greet a visiting dignitary, culminating in a stark warning not to shake hands as she would refuse this form of greeting. I accordingly looked serious and kept my hand by my side until I realised that she was holding out her own hand and beaming broadly, and so we shook hands and chatted through the evening. Quite why I had been given such advice, I never discovered.

Some years ago Olympic Airlines launched an advertising campaign, which sought to emphasise the 'O' of Olympic. Magazines carried a full-page advertisement with four photos of business travellers, three men and one woman in various forms of national dress, all holding out their right hand and making the O shape with finger and thumb. One of my students brought this to my attention in class, incredulous that a gesture deemed obscene in many countries could be used by an international company in a seemingly innocent manner. The ad disappeared not long afterwards, perhaps because others had drawn the airline's attention to their gaffe.

Driving round Ireland some 30 odd years ago with my Irish-American husband, I had to explain to him why people who had waved at us cheerily began shaking their fists when he responded with a V sign from behind the steering wheel. He was at first inclined to think it was the British number plates, but when I explained that making a V for Victory sign can be extremely derogatory if you hold your fingers in the wrong way, he calmed down and began to wave back instead.

In the Italian class, they were taught a variety of hand gestures, which included shrugging the shoulders, holding out two fingers to ward off the evil eye and the outstretched hands with arms close to the chest, accompanied by the interrogative 'Beh?' that can mean all sorts of things, but mainly that you do not consider what has just been said to be of any significance. My daughter was so good at these that a classmate asked her how she knew them all, and she replied that these were the gestures she had grown up with, Mum's gestures.

Yet, all those gestures come to me unconsciously. I am not aware of the gestures I make; they are so much a part of my life and my history. Not long after the children's language class, I was shown a video of myself at a doctoral examination in Finland a few years ago, waving my arms around like a windmill. Indeed, I did not just wave my arms, I rubbed my hands together in a sort of Uriah Heepish hand-wringing, and to make a point I would hold my arms out and then pull my hands back to the chest in a sort of embracing motion. It was fascinatingly horrible to watch and I wondered how many students over the years had been put off by what to them must have seemed bizarre gestural behaviour, all of which was completely unconscious on my part. What they made of this in Finland, where gesticulating is down to a minimum I shall never know, since my hosts were far too polite in their Nordic way to tell me.

Teaching the language of gestures while simultaneously teaching a foreign language seems to me admirable. If we are ever going to teach the significance of the extra-verbal, then this seems like a good way to start. Words are always spoken in a context, and the way in which they are spoken, accompanied by particular gestures adds to the layers of meaning in a communicative exchange. Understanding how other cultures operate is a vital part of translating and interpreting, and hence being able to read the sign language that accompanies (or replaces) words is as important as being able to translate the words themselves. It is also essential for a literary translator to be able to understand the significance of gestures described in a novel or indicated in stage directions, so as to find substitute gestures that could have more meaning for their audience if this turns out to be possible or to provide clarification if no equivalent replacement can be found.

Interestingly, gestures do not only vary across cultures, they also vary across time. Early 19th-century novelists like Mrs Gaskell or Charlotte Brontë who write with great sensitivity about the everyday habits of people as they observed them, record a variety of gestures that would not have the same meaning today. One often repeated gesture is the drumming of fingers on a table, either while waiting for another course to be served or while waiting for attention in a shop. This may well have been acceptable behaviour in polite English society in the 1830s but if anyone drummed their fingers on the table in my house while waiting for me to serve the pudding I fear they would not be invited back again. Such a tangible gesture of impatience would be seen as bad manners today where once it may have been unremarkable.

Learning to read different gestural languages is a vitally important stage in learning to understand, both verbally and physically, other cultures.

Teaching language learners about the way in which the native speakers of the language they are studying move and interact is as important as teaching them basic vocabulary and sentence structures. We may still get our Japanese bowing wrong, but at least we can learn something about the codification of bowing, and hopefully, we will learn not to insult the people with whom we are trying to communicate by making what to them are offensive gestures. Full marks to my children's teacher – I only wish all language teachers were as enlightened.

First published in *ITI Bulletin* January–February 2008.

Chapter 19
Just What Did You Call Me?

Because friends know of my interest in languages, sometimes unusual books arrive in the post. Last Christmas was no exception, and one of the most entertaining books I received was one with an extraordinarily provocative title. *Uglier than a Monkey's Armpit* by Robert Vanderplank (2007), Director of the Oxford University Language Centre, is subtitled *Untranslatable Insults, Put-Downs and Curses from Around the World*, and is a collection of bizarre insults, each illustrated with a comment by the author.

This is the sort of book that many readers will find amusing, once they overcome their resistance to dubious cultural stereotyping (e.g. Finns are not known for their wit, or Czechs have thicker skins than most people) Vanderplank has collected insults and assembled them under language headings. It is a very personal selection, presumably collected gradually from random sources. Some of the phrases he lists are obviously taken from literature, some are very obscure indeed, some are antiquated, others right up to date and some are in general use on a day-to-day basis. This mish-mash of different kinds of insult ensures that the book is entertaining with no pretensions to being encyclopaedic.

There is, of course, a serious aspect to insults and curses. In January 2008, the Indian cricket tour of Australia was nearly derailed over an insult. Harbhajan Singh was banned for three months, after being accused of insulting the Australian player Andrew Symonds. Singh apparently called him a monkey, which was taken as a racial insult, given Symonds' West Indian background. But writing in *The Daily Telegraph*, the BBC sports editor Mihir Bose offered another story about the insult. His version is that Singh did not call his opponent a monkey, but insulted him in Hindi, using the phrase *'There maa ki'* which, of course, could easily have been misheard as the English word 'monkey'. Ironically, this phrase which contains a scurrilous reference to Symonds' mother, Maa being the word for Mother, was so extremely offensive that the Indian team may well have opted for a word they felt was far less offensive, not recognising the racial overtones it carries in English. Bose argues that naughty children are often referred to as monkeys in India, so calling someone a monkey would not be particularly offensive. The case he constructs is indeed fascinating: here we have a cricketer who stands accused of making a racist remark, who may well have said something so profoundly offensive in another language that it was considered too embarrassing to translate. Yet in English, to call a black player a monkey is far more insulting than to use what has become an increasingly common phrase, a motherfucker.

I have always been fascinated by the ways in which different cultures conceive of insults, because unquestionably this is a culture-bound phenomenon. Some insults, when translated appear bland or slightly ridiculous. Strong insults referring to donkeys feature in many Middle Eastern contexts, but calling someone an ass in English is fairly mild. Blasphemous cursing in Italian or Spanish is puzzling rather than deeply offensive: *porca Madonna* is a horrible phrase, but an English speaker would have trouble grasping the degree to which it seen as unacceptable. Insults and curses do not translate easily, and even when they are translated the weight they carry with native speakers is very difficult to determine.

Vanderplank's book claims that his collection is untranslatable, and in one sense, this is true. 'He couldn't organise a piss-up in a brewery', one of the examples in the British-English section would indeed be hard to translate literally, and were anyone to attempt to do so, the result would be absurd. Similarly, a Hungarian phrase that roughly translated means 'looks as if he/she has been pulled through a hedge backwards', when translated literally becomes 'looks as if he/she has been pulled out of a cow's mouth.' J.C. Catford (1969), in his book *A Linguistic Theory of Translation*, written over 40 years ago but still extremely useful, discusses the absurdity of trying to translate adages or proverbs, phrases like 'it's raining cats and dogs' literally, and the same applies to insults. But when characters in a novel or a play insult one another, the translator has to find a solution that will work in the target language, and has also to find a solution that will render the degree of offensiveness with some precision.

One of the best illustrations of the need to determine the level of offensiveness of a word or phrase can be found in English. When Eliza Doolittle in Bernard Shaw's *Pygmalion* transformed into the musical *My Fair Lady* says 'Not bloody likely' and shocks the aristocratic society that she is trying to impress, she uttered a phrase that was indeed shocking for a lady in its own time. But once 'bloody' entered common parlance, the phrase ceased to have much impact and subsequent directors have 'translated' it into something more likely to shock later generations. I have seen at least two productions where Eliza has said 'Not fucking likely', though I predict that this too will need to be strengthened before long. Only last week, on a train, a small boy returning from a trip to London with his policeman father used the f-word with utter ease and neither Dad nor Grandad appeared to think it odd.

The question of weight is one that can be very troubling for translators. Take the word 'stupid' for example, which I use affectionately with my dogs all the time. 'Stupido' in Italian is much stronger, and were a character in an English play to call someone stupid, it would be best rendered in Italian as 'cretino', which is far less derogatory. When I tried to explain this to my son he was aghast: 'So in Italian it's better to call someone a cretin than just to tell them they're stupid, is it?' he asked, adding that it seemed quite wrong to him. The weight of an insult is one of the hardest ideas of all to grasp for the non-native speaker, yet it is crucial to both the insulter and the person insulted.

Some of the most interesting translation workshops I have run have been focused on blasphemy, obscenity and insult. Students have always brought fascinating examples, and I have learned a lot from them. Interestingly, some people found it much easier to speak a taboo phrase in translation, when the weight of the original words was diminished and made safer. Others could not speak the words at all; they were only willing to write them down, which testifies to the power of derogatory language in some cultures. Age, class and gender also play an important role in the use or non-use of certain words or phrases.

Different languages have developed different kinds of insult. Vanderplank tells us that Hungarian is the language in which obscenity appears most frequently. This surprised me, since I had always been told that Dutch and Afrikaans have an astonishing variety of obscene insults. Some cultures have developed the sexual obscenity, others the scatological, many have both. In his tantalisingly brief introductory paragraphs to each section, Vanderplank provides titbits of intriguing information, and he has obviously drawn to some extent on some of the literary traditions of cursing and insulting that still exist in many contexts.

Some would argue that offensive language is more widely used to day than in previous generations, but this is a misconception. In the 18th century, for example, right across Europe the range of insults was much larger, and insult competitions were a feature of many ale houses. There is a good reproduction of an early ale house insult battle in a novel by the American John Barthes, *The Sot Weed Factor*. The flyting, or exchange of insults in poetic form can be found in many cultures, most notably in the British Isles in the Scotland and which dates back to Anglo-Saxon and Norse origins. Colourful insults, curses and put-downs have often been regarded as expressions of particular talent, in the case of writers, story-tellers or comedians. One of my favourites is the curse uttered by Queen Margaret to the usurper king Richard III in Shakespeare's play of that name, when she refers to him as 'an elvish-mark'd abortive rooting hog', adding that he is the slander of his mother's womb, loathed issue of his father's loins, a 'rag of honour'. This is powerful stuff and the blank verse accentuates it.

But what about the story behind the monkey's armpit? Well, there is none really, except that apparently in Spanish, the more exaggerated the comparison, the more comical it sounds. The monkey's armpit comparison is peanuts compared to some of the insults Vanderplank has collected in his Spanish section. 'You can see less than a fish through his arse' is pretty colourful, but 'You're more stupid than peeing standing up' is an even more interesting image to conjure with. My favourite examples are in the Yiddish section, and include 'You should marry the Angel of death' and 'God should visit on you the best of His ten plagues.' Nicely poetic, well formulated and straight to the point – everything you want an insult to be in fact.

First published in *ITI Bulletin* March–April 2008.

Chapter 20
Lost in Translation

In September, I went to Galicia in Northern Spain, somewhere I have always wanted to visit, but somehow never managed to reach, though I got as far as the Portuguese border once and had spent a few days in Leon giving lectures. I wanted to go to Galicia, because I had never seen the shrine of Santiago da Compostela, and wanted to explore some of the prehistoric sites that are spread across that part of northern Spain.

Galicia is a fantastic region and I would recommend it to anyone who enjoys glorious, wild ocean views, walking up wooded mountainsides and seafood, in particular octopus for which the area is justly famous. But it is also an ideal place for a linguist to visit, for Galician is an Iberian language that is not Spanish and is not Portuguese, but is somewhere in between. These days bilingual signs are everywhere, which enables you to see clearly the extent to which Galician, or Gallego as it is known locally, diverges from standard Spanish. This is also an indication of the pride the locals take in their language, which was banned under Franco and is now undergoing a revival. Galicia hosts a Celtic festival every year, which brings together musicians from Brittany, Cornwall, Wales, Ireland and Scotland, the whole Celtic diaspora in fact, and there are strong parallels between all these regions in terms of their pride in a cultural and linguistic heritage that has had to struggle to survive against hostile central government policies.

I could write this whole essay about my discovery of Galicia and how fascinating that process of discovery is still proving to be, as I embark on reading Galician literature. But what I want to focus on is something else, which is certainly something that many readers will have encountered also, and that is the experience of travelling with someone who, apart from a bit of schoolboy French, is virtually monolingual.

Let me say from the outset that G. the person in question is a much-travelled man who is also an acclaimed travel writer, so what he brought to the trip was a keen sense of observation and an eye for detail. He has some schoolboy French and distant acquaintance with Urdu, but no knowledge of Spanish or Portuguese at all, so everything had to be translated for him. He was, it could be said, a terrific cultural observer, who often asked difficult questions that I struggled to answer, and once he realised that Galician was a distinct language in its own right, those questions often became very tough indeed. At what stage did the languages of the Iberian Peninsula begin markedly to diverge? Impossible to answer that one without a trip to the library. How exactly do they differ one from another – is it grammar, vocabulary, pronunciation or all three? I hazarded some semi-informed guesses, some of which were not hopelessly off the mark when I checked later, but my knowledge of linguistic history was decidedly shaky.

One lunchtime we were in a little village restaurant when a Portuguese couple came in and sat next to us. As the only diners in the room, we struck up a conversation. G. was intrigued to know how I could differentiate their speech from that of the Galician waitress because he could not hear any difference between them. When called upon to explain what I was hearing, I found it very hard to do. It is not easy to explain something you experience almost intuitively, so I tried to get round the question by asking him to think about regional variations of English, and about the relationship between English and Scots.

When you are the person who knows the language and your companion does not, you are inevitably the interpreter. Sometimes this is straightforward, such as when you ask someone for directions and then translate them for the person who is driving. Restaurant menus can be a great source of entertainment, particularly if you have the menu in the local language and he has the menu in execrable English and keeps asking you to explain the translation. But as the days passed, I found myself finding different ways of trying to convey some of the nuances of different conversations, so that G. could experience, albeit vicariously something of what I was experiencing, and I discovered that the way to do this was to find some sort of parallels in the language we both shared.

One afternoon we went to the village of Muxia, where there is a famous sanctuary to Our Lady of the Ship, located right next to the sea. There are some extraordinary stones, boulders to be more precise, along the shoreline just in front of the breaking waves, and two of these huge stones seem to be propping one another up, so that there is just space for someone to crawl under them at low tide. The Muxia shrine was built, according to the local tradition, on the site of an ancient prehistoric holy place, and is seen as one of several places in Galicia where Christian and pre-Christian rituals overlap. We were standing looking down over the great stones, when two middle-aged ladies appeared and deposited their bags on a nearby rock. Then one of them began to crawl under the two great boulders. We watched for a few minutes as she scrambled down, then crawled up and out again, before scrambling down once more to start the crawl again. Curiosity overcame me and I went down to have a closer look.

By the time I reached the boulders, the first lady was standing panting by the rucksacks, and the second was already engaged in the crawl. A young Spanish woman who had also been watching this, went up to them and asked what they were doing. The first lady explained, in colourful, highly expressive language, that I then tried to recapture in English for G. My version went something like this:

> We're here on a pilgrimage because these rocks do wonders for your back. You have to do it nine times, nine times mind, no less than nine times, and make sure you rub your shoulders on that bit of rock just down there. I came here last year because my back had been troubling me something awful, but since I did it, I haven't had the slightest twinge, no, not even a twinge, so I'm back again to make sure it stays like that. I used to have dreadful backache, I really suffered, I did, but since I did this I haven't felt even a twinge.

And she went on in this vein, repeating herself while her friend crawled under the rocks, then stopped for a short rest and told us she was finding it hard, she was, but she knew it would be worth it in the end, and the Spanish lady and I made encouraging noises. The talkative lady then told me I should try it too, and when I protested that I didn't suffer from backache, she looked surprised and said surely I had some pains I needed taken care of, and did I have headaches because there was another stone that did wonders for migraine. She indicated a boulder down by the water's edge where the waves were breaking, in which there was a head-shaped cavity. 'Just go over there and put your head nine times in that hole,' she advised. I declined on the grounds that it looked pretty dangerous. We were, after all, on the unfortunately named Costa da Morte and the breakers looked enormous.

What I was trying to convey in my English version was the liveliness of the lady's speech, her use of colloquialisms, her character, in short, and to do this I had to find an English parallel. I told G. to imagine two Coronation street characters, using particular turns of phrase and saying the same thing over and over again for emphasis.

Afterwards, when I thought about that incident, I wondered about the legitimacy of such a translation strategy. I had transposed the conversation into another culture altogether, and I had stressed the comic elements perhaps to the point of parody. But what I did not manage to convey was the conviction of the lady who claimed her backache had been miraculously cured by the stone, the seriousness that underpinned everything she was saying, a seriousness derived from faith. My rendering of what she said veered towards the humorous, because it was indeed a slightly comical encounter, but it missed the other dimension altogether because I could not find any parallels in English. Perhaps had I been Irish, where pilgrimages to shrines are not unusual, I might have been more successful.

All interpreters diverge in various ways from the source text, they all reshape and restructure, they gloss, add, omit, clarify and make all sorts of linguistic adjustments to ensure the message is adequately conveyed to the listeners. I did all these things at different times during our Galician trip, but it was when I came to translating conversations, that I found a performative element creeping in that involved using signs and codes that might help render what was being said more understandable to G. and give him some sense of who the speaker appeared to be.

A translation theorist would say that this is a classic example of acculturation: you make the foreign seem familiar by appropriating it into your own culture, and you find parallels that will appear meaningful to the listener who does not share your acquaintance with the source language and culture.

But in so doing, do you run the risk of diminishing cultural difference somehow? And in reinventing a character in another language when you attempt to translate a conversation, is that strictly fair to the original speaker? I have discussed these questions in lecture rooms for years, but somehow, the experience of talking to the ladies at Muxia and then trying to translate that encounter for G. has given me room for reflection.

First published in *ITI Bulletin* November–December 2008.

Chapter 21
Good Rhyme and Reason

The year 2007 started well for translation, with the publication of a new version of *Sir Gawain and the Green Knight* by the poet Simon Armitage. Reviewers have been enthusiastic about this book, and when I read it I could see why. Armitage has done a beautiful job of balancing the power of the story with the dynamic energy of the language, and has deliberately chosen an English that draws on his own northern vernacular.

The original author has been lost with the passing of time, since creating the poem somewhere in the last three decades of the 14th century. The text was also lost, for centuries, until a manuscript turned up again in the 19th century, and was published in 1839, since when it has been translated many times, including prose versions for children. J.R.R. Tolkien produced a version and the late Ted Hughes was working on his translation right up to his death. It is a poem that has never lost its appeal to readers, since it is extraordinarily colourful and exciting, and combines humour with magic, detailed description with strong dialogue held together with a tightly structured plot line.

The poem relates how a strange green knight appears one Christmas at Camelot and lays down a challenge to Arthur's court: he asks for a brave knight to cut off his head with an axe on the understanding that in one year's time that knight will seek him out and be prepared to receive a similar blow. Gawain obliges, and duly beheads the Green Knight who, far from being dead, picks up his own head and rides away with it. A year later, Gawain is on his quest to find the mysterious Green Chapel where he is to meet the knight when he comes to a castle and receives hospitality from the lord and his lady. Three times the lord rides out hunting, and while he is away the lady tries to seduce Gawain, who resists her efforts. The knight and he have agreed to exchange with one another whatever they have acquired during the day, so each evening the knight gives Gawain an animal he has killed and Gawain responds with a kiss that the lady has given to him. On the last day, the lady also gives Gawain a green girdle that she says will protect him from harm, and he conceals this from her husband. He then rides out to the appointed place and submits to the Green Knight's axe. But the Green Knight does not attempt to kill him and merely nicks the back of his neck, explaining that he is in fact the lord of the castle and the cut is a reminder that Gawain had not been entirely truthful about the green girdle. Overwhelmed with shame, because he has set his own self-protection above total honesty, Gawain rides back to Camelot where King Arthur decrees that the wearing of a green girdle will be a sign of nobleheartedness for everyone from then on.

The story of Gawain appeals on many levels, but for a translator what appeals above all is the language. The Gawain poet was from the North Midlands, probably from somewhere in what today is Cheshire, somewhere between the Wirral and the rising uplands of Derbyshire. Over the years, there have been claims staked by different places to the location of the castle and the green chapel, but there is nothing conclusive except the language itself, which is a very long way away from the London dialect used by Chaucer. Armitage is one in a line of fine poets like Hughes or Tony Harrison who have deliberately chosen to work with poems or plays produced in different varieties of medieval English. Part of the agenda here is to show that English poetry does not derive from any single linguistic tradition, and that the richness of regional variation and dialect could also be found in poetry, before the invention of standardised spellings and Standard English Pronunciation relegated such variants to the margins. He unashamedly states that part of his translation strategy has been to stress the northernness of the unknown poet's language, 'coaxing Gawain and his poem back into the Pennines' (Armitage, 2007). That strategy derives from how he perceives himself as a Northern poet, inevitably drawn to an earlier poet from his region. In his evocative, erudite book *The Idea of North*, Peter Davidson reminds us that '*Gawain* has been a crucial text in imagining the north for generation after generation of English readers' (Davidson, 2005).

Armitage is doing more with this translation than focussing on the poet's dialect, however. His decision to translate a medieval narrative poem puts him into the same camp as Seamus Heaney, whose version of *Beowulf* made the best-seller lists a few years ago. Armitage, like Heaney, Harrison and Hughes has used translation to give contemporary readers an insight into the lost world of the Middle Ages, a loss that is accelerating as fewer and fewer people find themselves able to read these works in the original versions of Old or Middle English.

When I was an undergraduate, Anglo-Saxon was compulsory, and we then progressed to Middle English writing. Some 30 years ago it was still assumed that students who had not had the kind of philological training of my generation would be able to read *Gawain* in the original, using an edition with good footnotes. When my eldest daughter did English A level in the late 1980s, Chaucer's *Canterbury Tales* was a set text. Today, you would look long and hard to find students reading English at university who would be able to read medieval works unless they were translated into modern English. What this means is that the English medieval literary heritage is vanishing as fast as Ancient Greek vanished in the early 20th century. Soon almost nobody under the age of 30 will be able to read any of it at all, and the role of translation will be vital to its continued survival.

The death of knowledge of medieval writing is not just a concern for scholars. The wealth of writing before the 16th century was huge, and exerted an enormous influence on subsequent writers. Watching a production of *Richard III* at Stratford recently, I was struck by the extent to which Shakespeare had drawn on characters and conventions of medieval drama to create his play. The whole canon of Arthurian legend was a medieval invention, as were morality tales, epic sagas of monster slaying and knightly quests, courtly love lyrics and tragic–comic mystery plays. I may sound like a dinosaur, but I am so grateful I sat through the early English grammar classes, because at least I have some access to that vanishing hoard of great literature.

Simon Armitage's decision to translate this poem is therefore an important milestone, both in asserting the variety of the English literary tradition and in ensuring that generations who have not been as lucky as their predecessors will be able to enjoy and benefit from works that would otherwise be closed to them. His translation technique reinforces that decision, for though he retains the alliterative form of the original with its pattern of stressed syllables, he does not shy away from using colloquialisms and contemporary language, just as the original poet used both high and low varieties of English in his poem. Here, for example, is his rendering of some of the lines describing the appearance of the Green Knight:

> Yet he wore no helmet and no hauberk either,
> no armoured apparel or plate was apparent,
> and he swung no sword nor sported any shield,
> but held in one hand a sprig of holly-
> of all the evergreens the greenest ever-
> and in the other hand held the mother of all axes,
> a cruel piece of kit I kid you not

The original version of the last two lines is

> and an axe in his other, a hoge and unmete
> a spetos sparthe to expoun in spelle, quo-so might

which can be literally rendered as

> and an axe in his other (hand)huge and monstrous
> a cruel battle-axe to describe in words, whoever tries to

Parts of the poem are immediately recognisable to the modern reader, as these two lines show, but 'spetos sparthe to expoun in spelle' requires a dictionary aid. Armitage has recognised this and in his introduction he says that he is most fascinated by those lines which almost make sense to the modern reader but not quite the majority in fact. He uses a lovely image to illustrate his technique as reader and translator:

> To the untrained eye, it is as if the poem were lying beneath a thin coat of ice, tantalizingly near yet frustratingly blurred. To a contemporary poet, one interested in narrative and form, and to a northerner who not only recognises plenty of the poem's dialect but who detects an echo of his own speech rhythms within the original, the urge to blow a little warm breath across that layer of frosting eventually proved irresistible. (Armitage, 2007: vi–vii)

The image of melting the ice to reach the poem beneath is a powerful one, and a reminder that the task of the translator is a vital part of the literary landscape. The translators of the *King James Bible* use images of opening windows to let in light or breaking the shell to get at the kernel within, but Armitage uses a wintery image, fitting indeed when the poem in question is set in winter, to illustrate his compulsion to translate this strange great poem. He has done a terrific job with this translation and maybe, just maybe, the strength of translations of poems such as this may entice even a few readers to make the effort and read in the original some of the great works of English literature that are at risk of being lost.

First published in *ITI Bulletin* March–April 2007.

Chapter 22
Women's Work

Recently I have been reading a new translation of the great Welsh cycle of 11 mediaeval tales, known collectively as *The Mabinogion*. I had read a version before, but this translation, published in 2008, is very good to read, probably because the translator has borne in mind the fact that the original tales were read aloud to an audience, and so she has tried to emphasise that performance aspect. The translator is Sioned Davies, professor of Welsh at Cardiff University, and in producing this new translation she has followed in the footsteps of an earlier distinguished female translator, Charlotte Guest.

Lady Charlotte Guest spent several years, from 1838 to 1846, translating the Welsh tales into English. Her great work included detailed scholarly notes and remained the standard translation for decades. Indeed, it can be argued that her translation brought Welsh mediaeval literature into the limelight at an important historical moment, when across Europe revolutionary movements were looking to their literary origins as a means of establishing their national identity.

Lady Charlotte did not grow up speaking Welsh; she learned it in later life, after her marriage, but was committed to using translation as a means of making known the greatness of what she perceived as a neglected literature. She is perhaps less well known than Lady Augusta Gregory, who brought Irish traditional songs and stories to the attention of whole new audiences inside and outside Ireland, but the task she set herself is a comparable one. Lady Charlotte clearly had a talent for languages, and taught herself some Arabic and Hebrew, before focusing her attention on Welsh.

When we start to look at the history of literatures in terms of translation, it is interesting to note the role played by women translators, whose work often had an enormous impact but whose contribution is often overlooked or whose names are often forgotten. One such female translator, whose translations had a huge impact on the English novel, was Constance Garnett, who produced an astonishing 71 volumes of translations from Russian. Her interest in Russian began when she was studying Classics at Newnham College, Cambridge, and grew over time. She travelled to Russia, meeting Tolstoy in 1893, and through her efforts a whole generation of English readers became acquainted with the great undiscovered literature in Russian. Yet when I have heard people say that they have read *War and Peace* or *Anna Karenina*, I never hear anyone mention Constance Garnett, without whom Tolstoy would have been inaccessible for decades.

A glance at the history of literary translation reveals a long list of names of gifted female translators. The Anglo-Saxon king, Alfred, who was one of the earliest translators, was instructed in the literary arts by his mother, and through the centuries there have been large numbers of educated, intelligent women engaged in translation. The Renaissance and Reformation saw many women undertaking the translation of ancient works and sacred texts, including Lady Mary Sidney and St Thomas More's daughter Margaret Roper. Elizabeth I translated throughout her life; at the age of 11, she sent her stepmother Catherine Parr a gift of her own translation of a work by the French queen Marguerite of Navarre, *The Glasse of the Synnefull Soule*. She enhanced the gift by placing it in a cover she embroidered with clusters of purple flowers. In old age she translated Boethius; translation for her was clearly an opportunity to engage with her own creativity, and it was probably also something that she enjoyed and found fulfilling, a welcome relief from affairs of state.

The question of why women should have begun to emerge as translators during the Renaissance has been much debated. One school of thought sees this as an indication of the low status of translation and of women themselves; women were allowed to translate because translation was seen as marginal anyway. An alternative view rejects this interpretation, arguing that translation in the Renaissance was anything but marginal, indeed translating was extremely significant – William Tyndale and Etienne Dolet were both burned at the stake on account of their subversive and heretical translations. The American translation scholar Douglas Robinson (1995) suggests that this was a period when women began to use translations as a means of giving themselves a public voice. Robinson calls this the 'feminisation' of translation, and his theory holds some weight when we look at the relationship between women and translating throughout the 17th century and after. Many famous women writers translated, from Aphra Behn to Mary Wollstonecraft, from Madame de Staël to George Eliot. Women translated plays, poetry, novels, philosophical texts and scientific treatises. Women were actively involved in commercial translation work from the 17th century onwards, supplying publishers with manuscripts translated from ancient and modern languages, and were particularly active in the 18th century in translating for the stage. In the 19th century, Karl Marx's daughter Eleanor translated Flaubert's *Madame Bovary*, a novel condemned for its immorality in France. Women in Victoria's England translated the scandalous Emile Zola and the shocking Ibsen. Translation appeared to offer an opportunity to women to break out of the traditional role of Angel of the House and speak through the work of another writer, often in radical ways.

One question that students ask perennially – I was asking it as an undergraduate, and it surfaces just as often today – is whether we can distinguish gender in writing. In other words, do men and women write differently, do they use language in different ways, can a reader faced with an anonymous piece of writing detect the gender of the writer regardless of subject matter? This question assumes particular importance when we think about translation, since we need to ask whether a work written by a woman can be adequately translated by a man and vice versa. Some feminist translators have indeed argued that the gender of the translator should match that of the original writer.

However, this approach is based on unstable and unproven assumptions about gender and writing and, furthermore, it limits the scope of a translator. There are some very fine translators, men and women, who simply produce good translations, regardless of gender issues. The late Giovanni Pontiero produced some beautiful translations of the Brazilian writer Clarice Lispector, while not only has Suzanne Jill Levine (1991) translated Latin American male writers brilliantly, she has also written with great elegance and wit about her translation strategies. Her book, *The Subversive Scribe: Translating Latin American Fiction* is a classic work that tackles the thorny question of gender identity through translation, looking at the problems that emerge when a feminist translator has to deal with misogynistic writing. In such circumstances, she argues, the translator becomes subversive, but then as she puts it, translating, like all forms of writing, involves a search for 'one's own language' (Levine, 1991).

Today there are a great many distinguished female translators. A full list would be impossible – there are some very fine translators, men and women, who simply produce good translations, regardless of gender issues – and any partial list is invidious, but a sample of names of translators whose work I have read with pleasure over the last couple of years include Margaret Sayers Peden, Amanda Hopkinson, Anthea Bell, Tiina Nunnaly, Ros Schwartz, Josephine Balmer, Carol Maier, Elaine Feinstein and Luise von Flotow, who work in different languages and genres, translating male and female writers alike.

Setting aside the question of the gender of writer and translator, there are nevertheless important issues that arise out of the different ways that gender is marked linguistically. Languages like English that do not have grammatical gender enable writers to play with ambiguity. The Spanish translator of the American poet Adrienne Rich found herself facing difficulties when translating some of Rich's love poetry into Spanish, for the beloved was another woman and consequently the language had to reflect that. Myriam Diaz-Diocaretz (1985) wrote a book about translating Rich's poetry, showing how the lesbian relationships that were implicit in English became explicit in Spanish because of the way the language works, and discussed how this caused problems in a society that was less tolerant of same-sex love affairs. In one of my own translations I once found myself having to give the sex of a baby from the outset, since the language I was working with would not let me keep the genderlessness of the word 'baby', which in English is neutral. Such decisions affect how a poem is read, but are unavoidable because the framework of the language in question demands it.

Some of the most thought-provoking and entertaining thinking about translation and gender has come from Canadian translators. I am particularly fond of Barbara Godard's (1990: 94) play on words when she writes about 'woman-handling' a text, which involves what she describes as the 'replacement of the modest self-effacing translator'. Translators like Godard and Levine have gone far beyond the question of whether translators should be of the same sex as the writers they are translating. Their emphasis is on the dynamic role of the translator, on the creativity of translation, on the fact that translating requires special skills and understanding, and is an act of recreation, since no translation can ever be identical to the original on which it is based. In this respect, as Sherry Simon (1996) succinctly puts it in her study of gender and translation, by emphasising translation as creative rewriting, assumptions about the supremacy of the original over the translation start to crumble away, just like assumptions about the supremacy of male over female, which opens the way for all translators, regardless of gender, to assert their own writerly authority and find their own distinctive voice.

First published in *ITI Bulletin* May–June 2010.

Chapter 23
Plays for Today

There is a rather good exhibition in the Shakespeare birthplace in Stratford-on-Avon, which I often take visitors to see. I took an English literature student there the other day, and was interested by his surprise at learning how Shakespeare actually wrote his plays. The exhibition explains a lot about Elizabethan theatre, showing how a writer like Shakespeare would have written parts for actors, similar to the *scenarii* of the commedia dell-arte players, and how those actors would have then developed the parts in their own special way.

What struck the student was that this was not how he had imagined Shakespeare at all: he had had the idea of a playwright sitting at a desk, a quill pen in hand, writing a complete play with acts and scenes, for throughout his school years he had been taught that Shakespeare was the greatest of all English writers and that his plays were close to perfection in the English language. To discover that in fact the plays were composed in fragments and that the texts which have come down to us are the product of centuries of editing was a great surprise.

When I was an undergraduate I thought the same, and I was always being told that the plays were not to be tampered with, they were whole perfect entities, the acme of English literature. As I grew older, I was increasingly thrilled by the exciting productions of Shakespeare that I saw in other languages, productions that often left standard English versions seeming rather dull. The theatre critic, Martin Esslin, who examined my PhD thesis (a wildly ambitious dog's breakfast of a dissertation on Einstein's theory of relativity on the European stage that thankfully has never seen the light of day!) told me a story that may be apocryphal, of the central European director who pitied the poor English, because they had to cope with Shakespeare in the original, and so were tied hand and foot to works of high status that could not be tampered with and, increasingly, could not be understood by the majority of the population. Those audiences privileged to have Shakespeare translated for them could enjoy the work of a writer who, as the late Polish scholar, Jan Kott proclaimed, was indeed their contemporary. The English may not be able to tamper with Shakespeare, but audiences in other cultures can enjoy new, innovative versions of his plays in translation.

I keep coming back to what I see as the problem of Shakespeare and translation, because it is fundamental in so many ways to how particular societies view both canonical works and the actual mechanics of translating. Regrettably, the English-speaking world does not have a very high opinion of translation, probably because English has been rising in global significance for several centuries, first as the language of colonialism, then as the language of the American (and subsequently Canadian, Australian and New Zealand dream) more recently as the language of global business and the internet. Given this history, it is hardly surprising that native English speakers should view themselves as uniquely privileged linguistically.

But a language that achieves success politically and economically cannot always claim the high ground indefinitely. The basic fact is that despite his talents, Shakespeare's language is increasingly inaccessible to English speakers and despite the canonical status of the plays, the truth is that they were never intended to be great literary works, they are a composite of speeches and scenes written piecemeal for talented and popular actors of the time. Hence the reason why in some cases the plot and characterisation lines do not seem to be coherent, as a famous Czech translator and director pointed out to me once. Sometimes characters behave differently from act to act, or plots change course rather oddly. Critics fret about this and often try to explain the discrepancies away, but once you stop and think about how the plays were put together, with parts written for actors, a degree of improvisation and later editing, inconsistencies are hardly surprising.

The theatre is, and always has been, collaborative. A lot of different people come together to make theatre – actors, technicians, writers, directors, designers and a host of others, including sponsors and patrons. The playscript is one element, and there are different kinds of play. There is the so-called well-made play, conceived of as a literary work, so that a playwright such as Luigi Pirandello or Arnold Wesker would expect actors to be faithful to the text and reproduce it in its entirety, learning lines by heart. There is the devised play, made by actors and directors such as Mike Leigh, where there is no fixed script, but rather a play fashioned collaboratively as the ensemble works together. There is the kind of play Shakespeare wrote, assembled in pieces and put together for eventual publication. What all these different kinds of play have in common is the fact that in order for the play to be realised in front of an audience, collaboration is required.

Translation scholars have often remarked on the lack of research into theatre translation, compared to other literary genres. An enormous amount of ink has been expended on discussing the translation of poetry and of prose, but not very much on theatre, and what remains is rather repetitive. Plays, we are informed, must be translated in order to be 'performable', though nobody seems able to explain quite what performability is. Small wonder, for criteria of performability have varied so radically over time and culture that there can be no consensus. In Shakespeare's day, all the performers were men, in Racine's day the actors wore high-heeled boots and minced around the stage while speaking in high-pitched unnatural voices. In the 19th century, actors struck grand poses and declaimed their lines like living statues. Plays written for different kinds of theatre clearly reflect different ideas about performability. And a play conceived of as a literary text will be very different from a play devised by a group of actors, possibly working with a jobbing writer.

The issues the translator of a play faces are complex. Crucial, however, is to recognise that the actual script is only one part of the total process that is theatre. The difficulty for the translator is that he or she has to deal with the written play, that is, with just one element of the whole. Isolated from the actual making of theatre, the translator can become deluded with dreams of grandeur and attempt to create a translation that does everything – renders the words into the target language, encodes signals that can then be taken up by actors and endeavours to be the director and the cast while sitting in front of the computer.

Shakespeare walked round on the boards handing out parts. No doubt the actors complained about some of what he had written and made him change their lines. That he was a genius as a writer is indisputable, but he wrote within the framework of the theatre of his day. Ideally, a translator today should do the same, and it is significant that where translators have been involved in production, they feel more empowered and do not rabbit on about performability and speakability and any other *-bility*, because they are not working in a vacuum but are actually, physically engaged.

Translating for the theatre is not like translating poetry or a novel; it is not and should not be solitary work. The collaborative nature of theatre means that ideally a translator should be engaged in the process, like the rest of the ensemble. This may well explain the success of Peter Brook's theatre, for example, where writers and translators do not work in isolation. Translators cannot know what an actor may find performable, they can only guess, yet once they can work with actors, revising and reshaping the words in performance, the play can acquire vitality and excitement. This is what happens to Shakespeare in languages other than English, when translators work alongside actors and directors to transform 16th century language into contemporary, meaningful idiom.

I am coming to the conclusion that the lack of translation theory specific to theatre is because the theorists erroneously thought of playwrighting as identical to the writing of poetry or prose fiction and endeavoured to fit their ideas of theatre into a restrictive mould. Translators of poetry or novels tend, like poets or novelists, to work alone. Translators of plays should not. They should endeavour to be involved in the business of theatre-making, because a good playwright will be doing just that. Racine's actors may have moved on the stage in ways that today we would find extraordinary, but he wrote his plays with the care of a choreographer, for precisely that kind of theatre. Today's translators of Racine cannot possibly reproduce that kind of writing, hence the need for them to work with actors of their own time and to shape their translation for the theatre of day. What keeps theatre alive is its capacity to renew itself. Translators for the theatre should be bold and collaborative and should remember that the image of Shakespeare at a desk writing a perfect finished play is nothing but a myth.

First published in *ITI Bulletin* March–April 2006.

Chapter 24
Between the Lines

Translation, as we all know, involves the transfer of words written in one language into another. Translators rewrite the words set down by the original author in a form that, ideally, renders that author accessible to a completely new readership. Generations of writers and critics have written about the difficulties of translating, and about the almost inevitable loss that occurs in the transfer process, while articles about translation are weighted down with words such as 'betrayal', 'infidelity' and 'untranslatability'. Despite this, however, translators go on translating and thanks to their efforts, we can all read works that would otherwise be closed to us because of our lack of necessary linguistic competence.

But translation is, as any translator knows, about much more than words. There may or may not be dictionary equivalents of words, phrases, idioms or proverbs but, as the French writer Mallarmé suggested, there is another text that exists between the lines of the one that we read and this is where the translator's skill is tested to the utmost. Translators have to work with so much more than just words, they have to work with silences and spaces between words, with the connotations that words arouse, with the nuances that readers can attribute to words.

Recently I was reading a collection of verse by the 19th-century Scot, William McGonagall, the man described by Punch as 'the greatest Bad Verse writer of his age'. McGonagall's verse is truly dreadful, the lines are of varying random length and do not scan, the choice of language is ludicrous and the pomposity of the poems has made them a comic favourite for generations of readers. His best-known poem is *The Tay Bridge Disaster*, and the first verse gives a good idea of how bad a poet McGonagall was:

> Beautiful Railway Bridge of the Silv'ry Tay!
> Alas I am very sorry to say
> That ninety lives have been taken away
> On the last Sabbath day of 1879,
> Which will be remembered for a very long time.

What would happen were anyone to translate McGonagall? Of course, all the usual problems of translating poetry would be encountered, such as what form to employ, whether patterns of sound can be reproduced, whether the imagery will transpose from language to language and so forth. But the principal problem is that this is such bad poetry, and the translator would need to ensure that the target language readers had a sense of why poetry written with serious intent should make people roar with laughter instead. McGonagall (self-styled 'poet and tragedian') chose noble themes – great battles of history, catastrophes such as the Tay Bridge disaster or shipwrecks, the deaths of eminent people, Queen Victoria's Jubilee, and turned them all into doggerel. The comedy comes from the imbalance between the seriousness of the subject matter and the banality of the language, between the attempts at rhyme and the writer's inability to handle the form he has chosen.

Recognising the comedy depends on readers having sufficient knowledge of good verse in order to recognise the bad. For the translator, this means acknowledging that there is a translation problem that goes beyond the words on the page and involves definitions of taste and aesthetics as well as prior knowledge on the part of readers.

I do not know if any brave translator has attempted McGonagall, whose writing offers challenges almost as great as those presented by *Finnegan's Wake*. Translators have certainly tackled works that involve equally difficult dilemmas. One such case is the work of Harold Pinter, one of Britain's most successful playwrights. Pinter's particularly English brand of dark comedy has been well received in many countries, but one aspect of his plays presents particular difficulties: his use of a recurrent stage direction, the single word 'pause'.

Some years ago, I went to a performance of a Pinter play in Milan. It was dreadful. Why? The pacing was all wrong. The translation appeared reasonable, the actors were experienced, but the pace of the production verged on the manic, so unlike the slow, measured, precisely timed Pinter productions I had seen in England, where the pauses serve to accentuate the lines spoken by the actors. It was during that production that I realised why I had also hated an Italian version of *Look Back in Anger*. The use of pauses and silences in the English original had been altered beyond recognition, and the result was a set of characters shouting at one another for the duration of the play.

Surely silence is silence anywhere, it could be argued. Pinter's stage directions can be perfectly well rendered in Italian or any other language if we are thinking only of lexical equivalents. There is a word for 'pause' and a word for 'silence' in Italian. The problem is that silences have different meanings in different contexts, and unless that point is grasped the end result for a theatre production will be a travesty. Silence in a social situation in Britain can involve embarrassment or, as Pinter so subtly demonstrates, menace or implicit threat. When silence falls abruptly around a dinner table in England, something has happened or is about to happen. When silence falls in the same context in Italy, something terrible has happened, and people rush in to fill the dangerous void.

In Finland, in contrast, silence can fall that is entirely comfortable. The first time this happened to me at a dinner in Helsinki, I was uneasy at first, but quickly learned that in Nordic countries silence can be socially acceptable and very pleasant. Sometimes it is good to eat quietly in the presence of friends without feeling that you have to make small talk to fill any gaps. The difference between a sudden silence in a social context in Finland, in England and in Italy is enormous, so great that it can almost be felt physically.

The point for a translator to note is that silence has completely different meanings in different cultures. Outside Europe, in Asian countries such as Japan, for example, silence can imply respect, and often silence has gender implications, with men speaking more frequently and loudly than women. The problem for a translator is to understand the different meanings of silence, and this is particularly important in the theatre. A playwright such as Pinter who uses silence in a culture-specific way is bound to be very, very different when performed in a context where silence is socially abhorrent or, equally, in one where long silences are socially acceptable.

Translating for the theatre is a complex activity and ideally one of collaboration between the translator, the director and actors. Questions of pace could, arguably, be left to the actors and the director, the translator's task having ceased once the script has been rendered in the target language. However, how are the actors to know that what Pinter means by the enigmatic word 'pause' might be something very different from their understanding of the word unless the translator manages to signal the distinction somehow? The role of the translator in such a case is not so much that of an interlingual translator, to use Roman Jakobson's (2000) terminology, but rather that of an intersemiotic translator, someone acquainted with different sign systems and able to mediate across cultural boundaries to ensure that adequate understanding can take place.

Translating Pinter and McGonagall offer the translator two tricky challenges. In the case of McGonagall, the temptation to improve his poetry in the target language would surely be strong. Either that or the opposite: the translator may try to create a parody of what in English is already parodic, for the joke comes from the awfulness of the verse that was written with serious intentions. Either strategy would risk failure. In the case of Pinter, or Tom Stoppard, another playwright who uses pauses and silences to great effect, the translator working in isolation might feel that there is nothing that can be done beyond word-for-word translation, then leaving the production company to work out what they want to do with the resulting play. But the translator working collaboratively should be able to mediate in such a way as to enable actors to recognise different cultural implications of silence. The task of the translator more often than not is indeed to translate the spaces between words, not just the words themselves.

First published in *ITI Bulletin* January–February 2004.

Chapter 25
Playing on Words

Since translation became a subject for serious study, scholars have tended to focus on literary translation, since it presents so many difficulties and possible solutions. There are hundreds of books and articles on the translation of poetry, even more books on the translation of sacred works, especially the *Bible*, and an unimaginable number of prefaces to literary works discussing translation. Yet remarkably little attention has been paid to one particular type of translation: that of the theatre. Indeed, some translation studies experts have described theatre translation as the 'Cinderella area' of their subject – the least researched and probably the least understood.

Europe on Stage: Translation and Theatre, a highly readable study of European drama on the English stage by one of the foremost experts in theatre translation, Gunilla Anderman (2005), talks about translation for the stage, not simply for the page. The well-known translator of plays from and into Swedish, who sadly died in April 2007, rightly perceived that there was a distinction between the two processes. Theatre is a form that comes into existence on several dimensions, and words are only one component. An experience of theatre involves listening and seeing, and can sometimes involve other senses as well.

The creation of a piece of theatre involves more than one person, and even a one-man show requires technical support and choreography. For the translator of drama there is, therefore, a tension between the public dimension of theatre, which involves actors, technicians, a playing space and an audience, and the private act of producing a script. It is this tension that has tended to put off translation scholars from formulating useful theories. What it has not put off, unfortunately, are translators who like to pontificate about how immensely 'performable' their version is, without clarifying what that might mean.

Trying to define how a play can be performable is very difficult. Sometimes 'performable' is used as a synonym for 'speakable', but what might be seen as speakable to a translator working at a desk in isolation may prove the opposite when attempted by an actor.

I have always believed that the task of the translator is to produce a script that can then be given to actors and that the translator should not try to second guess what an actor will do with it. What this means is that, ideally, translating for the theatre should be a collaborative activity, involving writers and translators, actors and directors. There is a mutual need for those who are experts in language and those who can transform language into physical experience to collaborate – those who go it alone do so at their peril.

A production of *The Seagull* by the Royal Shakespeare Company in 2007 received mixed reviews, with opinion divided about the text being performed. Rather than using existing translations of Chekhov's play or commissioning a completely new version, the director opted for a hybrid solution, whereby the actors themselves contributed lines and the play was shaped through rehearsal. That it became something that Chekhov might not have recognised was a point made by those critics who did not take to this strategy; the counter-argument being that this version was, at the very least, a version for 2007. One thing is clear: both the playwright and the putative translators appear to have been side-lined in an endeavour to produce a 'new' version.

Translations for the theatre seem to age more quickly than other kinds of translation. Part of the problem lies in the fact that, by taking into account so prominently the needs of an audience, the language into which plays are translated is usually very much of its own time. Given that language is dynamic and constantly changing, this means that a play dates more quickly than other genres. Having made a study of the translations of Luigi Pirandello, I can confirm that the translations of the 1920s were no longer appropriate for audiences in the 1960s and that the versions produced 30 years ago are no longer fit for purpose today.

Europe on Stage has a splendid example of a translation of Ibsen's *A Doll's House*, which was apparently so successful in its time that Harley Granville-Barker proposed that it be used as part of the drama school entrance exam for female students. Here is a sample of an exchange between Nora and her husband, in the version by T. Weber that so impressed Granville-Barker in 1880:

HELMER: Has my thoughtless bird again dissipated money?
NORA: But, Thorvald, we must enjoy ourselves a little. It is the first Christmas we need not to spare.

HELMER:	Know that we cannot dissipate.
NORA:	Yes, Thorvald, we may now dissipate a little, may we not?

Clearly, such a translation would be unusable today, but what is intriguing is that it ever had any validity, given the cringe-making quality of the language.

Another under-researched aspect of theatre translation involves the cultural dimension. Different theatre traditions have resulted in totally different norms and expectations, so German audiences, for example, will tolerate much longer performances than English audiences, where even classical writers such as Shakespeare have to be cut and tailored to fit the conventional two-and-a-half hours' playing time.

Different acting traditions require different ways of performing, with some theatres preferring physical theatre and others placing greater emphasis on vocal delivery; some actors trained to move at speed and others trained to take up poses and create tableaux. We can add today the impact of television on performance styles, and the difficulty that actors used to close-up work with a camera sometimes have when they step out on to a large stage.

All these factors influence translation, for a play written for one set of acting conventions may not be easily adjustable to another. This is certainly the case with Pirandello, who has never been very successful in English, though in contrast, Chekhov has been hugely successful, having been rewritten to fit English stage conventions and expectations.

Anderman notes these different theatre traditions, and highlights the problem for translators of culture-related allusions in plays. Writing about the lack of awareness of English life and culture among Swedish translators of Harold Pinter, she points out that audiences in Europe have nevertheless accepted what they do not understand (due to inadequate translations) as 'Pinteresque'. She goes on to speculate on what might have happened had Pinter been born in Finland:

> Would the cultural linguistic allusions made by this hypothetical North European Pinter, referring to national sports such as skiing and skating, Nordic folk songs, trolls and related mythology, have been described in reverent terms and referred to as 'Pinteresque', or would reviewers have been inclined to reach for other less flattering adjectives? (Anderman, 2005: 108)

Her argument is that failure to understand many of the cultural references and allusions in Pinter's work has served to turn him into more of a surrealist playwright than he may ever have intended. It could equally be argued that the transformation of Chekhov into a playwright whose main theme is nostalgia for a lost middle-class world stems from the failure of successive translators to map the complex Russian social system on to an English one. I still remember the first time I saw a Chekhov play in Russian and was stunned by its vitality, humour and vulgarity – a far cry from any productions I had seen on the English stage.

The reasons theatre translation has been so neglected by researchers working in translation studies are easy to see. Unlike a poem or a novel, a play is written as a kind of blueprint, a sort of precursor to its eventual performance, rather than as an end in itself. The task of the translator is therefore to render in another language something that is both a finished product – it is a play, after all – and a text that is a way-station on the journey to its eventual realisation on a stage. This means that the translated play is a rather extraordinary object, a double-blueprint as it were, existing as a translation both of a play written for performance in one context and of a text on the road to being performed in another.

First published in *The Linguist* 46 (6), 2007.

Chapter 26
Pleasures of Rereading

One of the pleasures of the summer is the possibility of having time to read. I always have a stack of books that I mean to read sooner or later, some of which I have to confess sit around for several summers, but in deciding what I am going to take on holiday with me I always make the conscious choice of at least one book that I have read before.

Years ago, my Great Aunt Mary used to tell me about the pleasures of rereading. She was quite systematic, and worked her way through some of the great poets that she had once taught to pupils aspiring to read English literature at university, along with a variety of her favourite novelists. When she died, she left me her library, and I inherited the complete works of writers from Henry Fielding to Anatole France, for Great Aunt Mary's tastes were fairly eclectic. She also, subliminally, must have left me the memory of her belief in rereading, because as I have come closer to the age she must have been when I knew her, so rereading has grown in importance.

When you reread, you discover afresh a book from your past. Sometimes that discovery is wonderful, because you realise how much you missed and, if you read it when you were too young to fully grasp what the author was saying, how much you failed to comprehend. Sometimes a book you think you knew well and perhaps have read several times changes in tone. It might seem more light-hearted than you remember or much darker. *Jane Eyre*, which I first read in my teens as a romantic tale and loved, disturbs me much more today, perhaps because I now know more about the poverty and brutality of the world Charlotte Brontë inhabited and captured in her writing. Perhaps my rereading of *Jane Eyre* has been changed forever by having read Jean Rhys' *Wide Sargasso Sea* which tells the story of Rochester's tragic West Indian wife, who, in Brontë's novel is merely the mad woman in the attic. *Madame Bovary*, the ending of which I find horrific, troubles me too, though I did not react like that when I was an undergraduate.

When a book you think you know affects you differently, it is a sure sign that it is not the book that has changed, but you. Perhaps you have become wiser, more sophisticated, or perhaps you are less arrogant, more open and able to empathise with the unfamiliar. Or perhaps your tastes have altered, perhaps you drink wine instead of beer these days and listen more to Mozart than to the Rolling Stones. Inner changes are even more apparent when you go back to a book you once thought was hilariously funny. It is rare to find that you still laugh at the same things 30 years later. This may not just be a question of personal taste changing however, for humour dates very quickly. Jokes and situations that are comic to one generation can be totally unfunny or even offensive to another generation.

So far I have been referring to books in general and making no distinction between languages. When we think about translation, however, the question of rereading assumes a very different significance, for every time we read a new translation of a work we have previously read, we engage in a more overt form of rereading, because each translator will reformulate the original in a slightly (or sometimes radically) different way. When I reread a Thomas Hardy novel, *The Return of the Native*, say, I am reading the same words, and however much my reaction to that novel may change over time, the words on the page are still the same words I have read before.

This is not the case when I read a new translation of a book like *Don Quixote*, for example. What I am reading now is a different version of Cervantes' novel, phrased by another translator for a 21st century public. The last time I read *Don Quixote*, in an English translation, was over a quarter of a century ago. John Rutherford is the translator of the present version, and he claims that the starting point for his new translation was his student daughter's complaints about how boring the novel was, so boring that she felt she would not get to the end of it. I sympathised with this story, since my own daughter said the same thing to me once, and the translation on offer on our bookshelves was indeed ponderous and dull, and if a translation fails to appeal, the reputation of the original suffers. John and I had the privilege of being able to read the Spanish, but our daughters were reliant on a translation. He duly set about translating the great work, primarily for his daughter, only to find, when he had finished his first draft, that two other distinguished translators were also producing versions. Undeterred, he continued, determined to produce a translation that would give contemporary readers some sense of how funny Cervantes' novel must have been for his contemporaries, using his daughter as a yardstick to gauge his degree of success. The result is, in effect, a funnier English version than the one I had read previously, and one which John's daughter rated a success.

The fact that three translators all chose to work on *Don Quixote* on both sides of the Atlantic at the same time also tells us something about changes of taste and rereading. Clearly, both publishers and translators felt that there was a need to retranslate Cervantes for the new millennium. Interestingly, all three published with slightly different titles: John Rutherford opted for *The Ingenious Hidalgo. Don Quixote de la Mancha*, Burton Raffel for *The History of that Ingenious Gentleman Don Quijote de la Mancha* and Edith Grossman for the plain *Don Quixote*, which is the standard English title by which Cervantes' novel is known.

Although translations are continually being remade, there are norms and expectations that can help to determine success or failure. If a title is well established, changing it can perturb. The recent debate about whether *The Karamazov Brothers* is a more 'accurate' rendering of the Russian is a non-argument, since English language readers know the novel as *The Brothers Karamazov*, and the slightly strange word order, with its Biblical undertones, serves to mark the novel out as distinctive and special. There is a banality to *The Karamazov Brothers* even though it is both a more modern and more literal rendering of the Russian. There were similar debates about the English translation of *A la recherché du temps perdu*, about whether *In Search of Lost Time* had the same impact as Scott-Moncrieff's 1920s title, *Remembrance of Things Past*.

Readers who have never translated anything nevertheless know what they want from a translation if it is of a work that they have read before. The title offers a kind of guarantee, and to change that title calls into question the authenticity of the translation itself. The mediaeval Arabic stories published in French in the early 18th century as *Les Mille et une nuit* emerged in English shortly afterwards as *Arabian Winter-Evenings' Entertainments or Arabian Nights' Entertainments*. The 'Arabian Nights' element took hold, and several subsequent translations had to add the phrase, as for example did Sir Richard Burton in his ponderously titled translation *The Book of the Thousand and One Nights: A Plain and Literal Translation of the Arabian Nights' Entertainments*. Robert Mack's 1995 Oxford translation was simply titled *Arabian Nights Entertainments*. English readers had become more familiar with the idea of the Arabian nights than with the thousand and one nights.

Translations are rewritings, in that they are new language versions of something written originally in another language. Translations are also physical manifestations of the translator's readings of that original, and it may be that if we are familiar with a work through a particular translation, we find it difficult to respond positively to changes. If we react differently when we reread a novel by George Eliot after 20 years, we can perhaps agree that this is because we are reading through different eyes. But if we react differently when we read a new translation of *Père Goriot*, we attribute the difference to the translation, not to changes within ourselves, even though we are claiming to be rereading Balzac's novel.

What this difference in readings shows is how much we rely on translators to give us what we feel is familiar. Changing a title, or changing the emphasis of a work offends us in a translation, while we accept that our memory may have deceived us if we fail to discover what we thought was there when we reread something we read a long time ago. Does this mean that readers of translations are more conservative than other readers, or is it just that new translations compel us to recognise that the world keeps changing?

First published in *ITI Bulletin* September–October 2008.

Chapter 27
On the Case

I have to confess that I was never a fan of crime fiction. I enjoyed the occasional film or TV thriller, but the detective novel always left me cold. I knew Inspector Poirot through David Suchet's performances, since I had never read anything by Agatha Christie, just as I had never read a Father Brown novel, nor a Cadfael novel, nor anything by Ruth Rendell or Henning Mankel. Friends and family have praised various writers and recommended them to me over the years, but I never followed up their suggestions.

Until now, that is. Belatedly in life, I have become an avid reader of detective fiction and am currently working my way through the cases solved by Adam Dalgleish, P.D. James' poetry-writing detective. As an occasional change of pace, I am also reading Dorothy Sayers, entertained by the problem-solving cases of Lord Peter Wimsey, and I have to confess that I am gradually becoming a serious aficionado of this kind of writing.

How this change has come about, I am not sure, but it most certainly has something to do with translation. A few years ago, when I was one of the judges for the Independent Foreign Fiction Prize, I found myself having to read a whole range of detective novels originally written in French, Spanish, Dutch, German, Swedish and Italian, novels that were often compelling and worked on several different levels. Many of the novels had a conventional murder mystery plot, but as the story unravelled, so a more politicized dimension could often be seen. Complex story lines led back to the post-war period in Europe, to the Franco or Salazar era, to the Holocaust, to the Balkan wars of the 1990s. Beneath the fabric of contemporary society, dark secrets that had been hidden for years seeped out into the daylight, secrets that in some novels tore families or whole communities apart. Solving a contemporary crime in some of those novels involved delving into the past, where other different crimes had been committed and covered up. Getting at the truth in time present also involved being honest about the past and facing up to suppressed personal traumas.

The story of a secret crime passed down from another generation is a powerful theme of many contemporary European crime novelists, and, in a less overtly politicised context, is also at the heart of a great deal of crime fiction, on page and screen in North America. The cold case, where a team investigates a crime committed a decade or so earlier is so popular right now that there are several series of forensic programmes running on TV in the United States, Britain and other European countries. Indeed, so popular is the idea of forensic science as a way of resolving unsolved crimes that there is an unprecedented interest in this subject at university level, with dozens of students interested in what has suddenly become a glamourised profession in forensics. In a few years time, someone will look back on this early 21st century phenomenon and speculate on why this should be happening. Might it be that novelists like Patricia Cornwell and the writers behind TV programmes like *Bones* on both sides of the Atlantic are somehow raising questions about the origins of the values of our rich, yet fear-laden post-9/11 society?

British crime writers such as P.D. James and Ruth Rendell have both been made peers of the realm, honoured because of the phenomenal national and international success of their writing, and, like Agatha Christie and many other writers of this genre, both have been extensively translated into many languages. Today, though, there is arguably a boom in detective fiction internationally, a boom reflected in the growing number of translations into and out of English. Peter Hoeg's best-selling novel, *Miss Smilla's Feeling for Snow*, translated by Tiina Nunnally, introduced a talented Danish writer to a worldwide readership, and so popular have Henning Mankel's Kurt Wallander novels, translated by Laurie Thompson and Steven T. Murray, become that there has been an increase in tourists visiting Southern Sweden to see the places where the Swedish detective solves his cases. Wallander made his first appearance on British television this November, played by Kenneth Branagh. Anyone doubting the proliferation of gifted crime fiction writers across Europe should take a look at www.eurocrime.co.uk where hundreds of authors are listed.

The fact that there should be an international boom is also a testament to the skills of the translators of detective fiction, for this is a genre that has special characteristics which make demands on the translator's expertise. One of the features of much detective fiction is an emphasis on detail, for a skilful writer often plants clues in the detail, thereby compelling readers to pay attention to what might, in other types of text, be mere background information or scene setting. The descriptive passages can be as important, perhaps even more important than dialogue; what I have found since I started my detective fiction reading extravaganza is that I am gradually being led to read differently, to pay attention to minutiae, to question why a writer has provided or left out certain details, in short, to read as an active agent in the case-solving process.

Yet this kind of writing is also heavily culture bound. Small details make sense to people who can decode their significance – a certain kind of china tea cup might tell an English reader something about the background of the character who drinks from it, a detail that would be lost on a reader from a culture unfamiliar with the complexities of the British class system. Yet if that tea cup is a vital clue in solving the mystery, then the translator needs to find a way of signalling its significance, though obviously without highlighting it too heavily, risking patronising readers. So, for example, when the body of an artist is found close to a landscape painting that we are told 'showed a morning lighting', in Dorothy Sayers' classic *The Five Red Herrings* we are given a detailed account of the dead man's palette of paints, and the contents of his satchel, so that we learn that he used vermilion, ultramarine, viridian, cobalt, rose madder, crimson lake and lemon yellow, and we learn also that Lord Peter Wimsey is dissatisfied because something appears to be missing. What is missing is the flake white paint that the killer failed to leave behind, the vital clue that leads to his exposure. The key, of course, lies in the fact that morning light in Scotland could not be adequately rendered through the use of the strong colours discovered at the scene of the crime, hence the painting must have been done by someone other than the dead artist.

In her fascinating book *Culture Bumps*, Ritva Leppihalme tackles one of the most complex problems facing a translator, those elements of a text that are culture bound. She focuses her attention on allusions, in Finnish and English, and as she was researching this project she came to see that detective fiction seemed particularly high in allusive material. Her corpus consists of a variety of different texts, and she considers some of the strategies used by translators to render culture-bound material in another language and discusses the relative difficulty of translating different kinds of allusion. A biblical allusion might be relatively straightforward, since there are versions of the *Bible* in both languages, a Shakespearean allusion is more difficult, though there is a classic Finnish translation, However, far more complex are allusions to *Kalevala*, the Finnish epic that is almost unknown to English readers, or the following passage from Ruth Rendell's *To Fear a Painted Devil*:

> Nancy could hardly believe a letter would make her so happy. '... She is nothing to us. We each possess one world. Each hath one and is one.' Hath, she decided, must be a typing error, but the thought was there.

Hath, of course, is not a typing error at all, for the allusion here is to John Donne's poem, 'The Good Morrow', an allusion that would be lost on English readers unfamiliar with the poem, and totally lost on Finnish readers were it to be translated literally. The only way forward for a translator here is either to omit the allusion altogether or to find a substitute from Finnish literature that might serve a similar purpose.

Leppihalme suggests that authors who use allusions extensively, and this is indeed the case with many crime fiction writers, are establishing a special relationship with their readers, what she terms an in-group, 'with the reader flattered at being included'. This is an interesting idea, and might go some way towards explaining why certain kinds of writing and certain authors who follow a particular formula often attract a strong following. It is not just the character of a particular detective, nor the skilful unfolding of a complex, twisting plot line, but actual stylistic devices that are both hermeneutic on one level and designed to capture the attention of a certain kind of reader on the other.

What this means is that it takes a translator with a particular kind of ability to make a success of translating a genre that is full of puzzles both in form and content. Solving mysteries can take place both in terms of plot delineation and in terms of stylistic decoding, and more and more translators seem able to take on this task, thereby bringing some fine writers hitherto not familiar to English readers to our attention. David Hackston is the translator of the Finnish crime writer, Matti Joensuu (1997) and though I am unqualified to comment on how well he may have rendered Joensuu's Finnish style, the English result is well worth reading. Having discovered a taste for a genre that had until lately passed me by, I have now learned what I have been missing and have a new respect for what is often complex and multi-layered writing. Thanks to some excellent translators, I can now also extend my reading beyond the more traditional boundaries of the English-language world. I foresee a great many entertaining and enthralling evenings stretching out ahead of me.

First published in *ITI Bulletin* January–February 2009.

Chapter 28
Gained in Translation

At a dinner table the other week the conversation moved on to a discussion about translation. One of the people round the table was very dismissive – never yet read a good translation, you have to recognise that something is always lost in translation, better by far to read the original. Well, yes, countered someone else, but what if you do not know the language, and surely since nobody can know every language, it is not going to be possible to do without translations altogether? The pundit was unfazed by this argument: he avoided translations because they were always poor, you could always tell when a book was translated because there was always something missing, translations were deficient stylistically.

I did not let myself get too involved because this sort of argument irritates and depresses me. Of course things are lost in translation, of course a translation is not the same as the original, but that does not mean that someone reading that translation will always be short-changed. A good translation takes the reader into the world of the (translated) book in the same way that a writer took his or her readers into the original book in the first instance. There is loss in translation, but there is also gain, and this elementary fact seems so often to be forgotten.

What is also often forgotten is that for a translator, the act of translating is probably the most thorough of all ways of reading a text. A director will read a play with an eye to staging it, actors will read the same play focusing on their roles, literary scholars will read looking out for hermeneutic patterns and codes, reviewers will read scanning for something to praise or condemn, but a translator reads every word so as to gain as full an understanding of the work as possible before embarking on the task of decoding it, and then reshaping it in another language for new readers.

When I translate a poem or a play or a novel, I scribble a basic version as fast as my hand will move across the page and yes, I said hand, because I do my first drafts the old-fashioned way, writing with a pen on paper. Every time I encounter a glitch, which can range from not understanding a word to being ambiguous about how best to render it, I put brackets round it and keep on scribbling. I do not pause to look anything up, because that first draft is actually a written record of a reading, the reading that will form the basis of my final version.

The result of this first phase of working can be pages of almost indecipherable scrawl, but from that crude draft I can see all sorts of interesting things that I would not have seen had I not been trying to write in English almost simultaneously with reading the text in another language. I can see structural problems, issues that will have to be resolved but which will take a lot of effort to render adequately for readers, I can see passages that flow well and will sometimes go into the final version unaltered apart from a bit of tweaking here and there, and I can sometimes see places where the original 'wobbles', where perhaps even the original writer did not have full control over his or her writing at that point. Hardest of all are those points where the writer is deliberately ambiguous, which forces you to make hard choices if the ambiguity cannot be rendered in the target language.

What annoys me about people who condemn translations as second-best, as somehow lacking in some vital way, is that they clearly have no sense of the involvement of the translator, who is simultaneously reader, editor and (re-writer). I use the word 'editor' deliberately, for translation does indeed involve taking decisions that can only be described as editorial. I once left out several lines of a Renaissance Latin poem because I judged that the densely packed classical references in those lines would be so obscure for contemporary readers that their reading of the poem would have been impaired had I left them in. However, this was an editorial decision taken in clear knowledge of where the poem was destined to be published, which was in an anthology of women's poetry on the environment throughout the ages. Had I been translating the same poem for a scholarly edition of the poet's work, I would have left those lines in and backed them up with footnotes. For general readers, though, I was working on the assumption that the scholarly footnote is off-putting. As a reader, I am most certainly put off by excessive footnotes even though I appreciate them when I am engaged in a different kind of reading, one that relates to my research.

There is also another kind of translation reading, however, and that involves translating in order to get to know a writer more completely. Perhaps because I have worked for so many years in translation, I find that translating can actually be a valuable way of coming closer to a poet writing in a language I can read. This has been happening to me lately with the Spanish poet, Antonio Machado.

Many years ago I translated some of Machado's poems, working with an old friend, Salvador Ortiz-Carboneres, who was to go on and publish a collection of Machado's poetry, co-translated with Paul Burns in 2002. What I saw in Machado, as I saw in Unamuno, a poet we also worked on together, was the tantalising challenge of the combination of apparent simplicity and extraordinary spiritual depths. Take this one verse from a poem dedicated to an elderly Castilian poet, Narciso Alonso Cortes:

El alma. El alma vence- ! la pobre cenicienta,
que en este siglo vano, cruel, empedernido,
por esos mundos vaga escualida y hambrienta!-
al angel de la muerte e al agua del olvido.

Literally rendered, this reads as follows: The soul. The soul conquers- the poor Cinderella/ who in this empty, cruel, stony age/ through this world wanders wretched and hungry/- the angel of death and the water of oblivion.

The language of this verse, like the rest of the poem, is relatively straightforward. Of course a translator can play around with adjectives – *vano* could be empty, vain, futile, *escualida* could be wretched, thin, miserable and so forth, but the strength of the verse relies on the structure, which focuses on the word *alma*, repeated twice in the first line. *El alma*- the soul is separated from the rest of the verse by a full stop, which instantly highlights its importance. The second sentence repeats *el alma*, this time with the verb – *el alma vence* – the soul conquers/ triumphs, overcomes, a hugely powerful statement, which is then immediately broken by the central lines of the stanza that describe the misery of the soul. It is not until the final line that we learn what it is that the soul has triumphed over: the angel of death and the waters (plural in English, of course) of oblivion. The first and last lines are thus held together in a state of heightened tension, creating a bowstring effect. This is a technique that Machado uses frequently, but it confronts the translator with a problem to solve: English syntax is different from Spanish, and the tension cannot be sustained if the verb stays in the first line, because the object of that verb is too far away for full impact.

So what can be done: Stanley Applebaum in his 2007 version moves the verb 'conquers' to the start of the last line. This is fine, but it separates the soul from its verb, so that the sense of the all-powerful soul is diminished because the phrase *el alma vence* has been split. An alternative would be to move the second soul with the verb, so that the first line would read: 'The soul! That poor Cinderella-' and the last line would begin 'the soul triumphs over ...'

That would keep something of Machado's emphasis, but would make for a somewhat ungainly stanza in terms of length of lines.

Whatever solution the translator comes to, what is undeniable is the difficulty of translating a writer who appears on the surface to be accessible, and who indeed *is* accessible, since the beauty of his poetry is obvious to anyone who picks up one of his books, but whose poetry functions on different levels. Machado is a poet who is both profoundly spiritual and in possession of an astonishing pictorial ability that enables him to create images of the Spanish landscape that have made him one of the best-loved 20th century poets in his homeland.

As I go on scribbling crude versions of Machado's poems, the complexity beneath the apparent simplicity becomes more and more evident. I am gradually getting to know Machado better, and perhaps eventually I might venture to try and polish some of the scribbles into readable versions. For now, though, I am appreciative of the work of other translators who have been bold enough to tackle this marvellous, difficult, most readable of poets.

First published in *ITI Bulletin* March–April 2009.

Chapter 29
Layers of Meaning

One of the best-known poems in English must surely be Keats' *Ode to Autumn* which begins:

> Season of mists and mellow fruitfulness
> Close bosom-friend of the maturing sun;

It is a hymn to a particular moment in the English year, not to the autumn of chill winds and falling leaves, but to that period of transition when summer reaches its apogee, and hints of another season can be felt in the air. Keats sketches that moment, noting the ripe fruit, the bees who 'think warm days will never cease', the clouds of gnats over the river, the song of the crickets in the hedgerows, the harvest and the cider-making. And every year I think of that poem when I experience such days, for despite global warming some of the basic weather patterns have not changed, and there comes a time, usually in August, though this year in September, when you can see and feel everything Keats describes in his poem, right down to the last line, 'And gathering swallows twitter in the skies', for indeed the swallows do gather in this season. The one difference from Keats' day is that they now line up on telephone wires!

Now the point of giving this example is to ask what translators make of this kind of natural description, which is so intimately bound up with a particular geographical region. Keats' season of mists and mellow fruitfulness can, in all likelihood begin early in August, and certainly by the end of August the nights are lengthening, so that by mid-September it feels as if the darkness is gathering momentum. Once this happens, conversations in my local shop often revolve around a lament for the absence of summer, for the summer we seemingly have never had.

Only of course we *have* had a summer, it is just that our Northern summer started months ago, when the weather was still chilly, for summer in this country revolves not around warmth so much as around light. The anonymous mediaeval poet who composed the song 'Summer is i-cumin in' wrote about bird song, the call of the cuckoo, the growth of new leaves and the birth of lambs and calves all of which come relatively early in the year with the extended hours of daylight. The longest day comes in June, when the temperature is still only starting to heat up, and after that, through the hottest days of July and August there is a steady slide back towards the dark.

It took me a long time to adjust to the idea of summer being more about light than warmth, and so reaching its high point and then ending earlier than in much of southern and central Europe. Even now, I find it disconcerting to come back from a southern European country in early September, where the summer season is slowly ending but where the sun is still hot and the trappings of summer holidays are all around me, to a context where summer has already metamorphosed into autumn and the darkness is building. Eugenio Montale, who captures the essence of summers in Italy so marvellously writes about the land 'dove il sole cuoce/e annuvolano l'aria le zanzare', (where the sun broils/ and clouds of mosquitoes fill the air), where snakes rustle through the undergrowth beside garden walls too hot to touch. This is not a summer that is determined by light, but a summer conceived of as heat, so intense that since ancient times those who could afford to do so have left the heat of the cities and retreated to the hills. Summer in the south means seeking escape from that heat, it means keeping shutters and windows closed to try and keep the house cool, it means resting indoors in the hottest time of the day, it means fields of brilliant sunflowers (one of Montale's most famous poems is about sunflowers) like those painted by Van Gogh in Provence.

Nothing like that in the northern countries, where summer means long hours of daylight, so that you can sit outside until 10 o'clock, it means weekly grass cutting, harvesting roses and soft fruit, opening windows and taking buckets and spades to the seaside where, if you are hardy enough, you might venture into the sparkling grey sea. The word summer, for which there are dictionary equivalents in all the major European languages carries such very different sets of connotations and means different things to different cultures.

The changing of seasons has provided inspiration for writers all over the world for generations, but faces translators with all kinds of difficulties. We may understand the literal meaning of the word 'monsoon', but if we have never experienced it we cannot understand the particular emotional state that comes with the onset of the monsoon, or the reactions to its delay or absence. Someone used to the abrupt plunge into blackness when the sun goes down in the tropics may have some idea of what twilight might mean, but no real sense of the emotional significance of that time of day in a culture where the hours of in-betweenness, neither day nor night hold great symbolic power. I did not understand what it means to experience perpetual daylight until I spent a week in Reykjavik in mid-summer and the milky white light never varied in the slightest, day or night, which was very disorienting.

I once translated an Italian novel about a love affair between an older woman and a younger man, she the personification of Autumn, he of Spring. The story begins in a golden, steamy late summer evening in Venice, with descriptions of the bronze-coloured water, the heavy scents drifting down from gardens and the sunlight of what was termed 'Titian's hour' when the rich colour palette of that Venetian Renaissance master comes to life again in the stones. Later, as the young man's passion begins to fade, descriptions of the warmth and light give way to the chill, damp fogs of the Venetian hinterland. The difficulty I had was one encountered by many translators: how to put across the different layers of meaning for readers who had never experienced the seasons in the way d'Annunzio described them.

A classic translation problem is still Homer's 'wine-dark sea', a phrase that recurs through *The Iliad*. Commentators have written reams about what this might mean, some claiming to have seen purplish water, hence seeking a literal meaning for the phrase, and suggesting that this is a phenomenon specific to the Eastern Mediterranean at certain times of the year. But for most of us, the sea is shaded in greys, blues, greens and turquoise, brown sometimes where sand or river silt is stirred up, it is never dark red, never wine-coloured. Homer's phrase remains evocative of something mysterious and not quite understood.

Of course I am not suggesting that in order to translate you have to have direct experience of whatever it is you are translating. This has never been the case and would be absurd. Besides, these days, with visual images available at the touch of a button, we do not even have to try and imagine other seasons and places. But the examples of seasonal differences highlight one of the great problems of translation, which is that although some words and concepts may be easily rendered in other languages and have their dictionary equivalents, what is not translatable are the additional layers of meaning that are embedded in a particular culture. Anyone who thinks translation is just about words must think again, for translation so often involves far more than words themselves.

An English teacher from New Zealand told me about the difficulty she had convincing her pupils that the poetry they were reading about spring happening in April made sense. In Northern Europe, the daffodils do start to flower in March and by April, spring is so advanced that Browning could write longingly about wanting to be back in England at that most beautiful time of the year. But in the southern hemisphere the daffodils bloom in September, while in April the leaves are falling and winter is on its way. How then to understand the symbolic significance of T.S. Eliot's lines 'April is the cruellest month breeding/ Lilacs out of the dead land' or Shakespeare's ironic 'men are April when they woo' without engaging in what can only be called cultural translation?

Homi Bhabha (1990), the scholar who is most associated with cultural translation, uses descriptions of the weather to illustrate the difficulties of negotiating between cultures. Invoking images of English weather, he argues,

> Encourages memories of the 'deep' nations crafted in chalk and limestone: the quilted downs, the moors menaced by the wind, the quiet cathedral towns, that corner of a foreign field that is forever England. The English weather also revives images of its daemonic double: the heat and dust of India, the dark emptiness of Africa ... (Bhabha, 1990: 319)

One set of stereotypes calls forth another set of very different stereotypes, which Bhabha suggests were seen as strange and undesirable ones by people setting out to such places. The point he is making is interesting because he touches on the great mass of meanings, symbolic and actual that people come to attach to aspects of their cultures, and few aspects of any culture are more obvious than the weather.

The great challenge of translation is that so much is elusive as we cross language boundaries, but at the same time that is what makes translation so exciting. And if we translate well, then readers can have insights into other worlds and be enriched in consequence.

First published in *ITI Bulletin* November–December 2009.

Chapter 30
The Value of Comparing Translations

Any translator who takes on a text that has been translated before will almost certainly want to look back and see how another translator has tackled the same work. Some translators avoid doing this until after they have produced their own version, so as to avoid the risk of copying, even inadvertently, but others start with the previous version and so set out deliberately to produce something different. Once a work has been translated, subsequent translators are producing versions not just of the original, but of preceding translations.

Comparing translations can reveal all sorts of things. We can see how different translators have worked, what strategies they have employed and what choices they have made, and also how tastes alter over time and how readers' expectations vary.

When a work has been translated many times, comparing translations gives us insight into the history of translation practice.

Some translations become canonical, and cannot be bettered. A case in point is Edward Fitzgerald's *The Rubaiyat of Omar Khayyam*, which has held its own since it first appeared in 1859. In 1967, Robert Graves and Omar Ali-Shah produced another version, which they claimed was far closer to the original poem. Fitzgerald, they argued, had inadequate knowledge of both the Persian language and the Persian culture, and his translation was a travesty of the mystical source. They may have been right, but their translation failed to have any impact on English readers. Fitzgerald's translation, travesty or not, had acquired a place in English literature and no alternative version could supplant it.

The American translator Eliot Weinberger (2002) is wonderfully articulate about translation. In a recent essay he points out that above all else, translation involves change. 'Translation', Weinberger argues, 'is movement, the twin of metaphor, which means "to move from one place to another"' (Weinberger, 2002: 110). Metaphor is a process that makes the familiar appear strange, while translation does the opposite and makes the strange seem familiar. Both are processes of change that take the reader into new dimensions.

One of my favourite books on translation is Weinberger's (1987) *Nineteen Ways of Looking at Wang Wei*, subtitled *How a Chinese Poem is Translated*.

In this superb comparative study of translations, Weinberger presents a series of different versions of a four-line poem by the Chinese master poet Wang Wei (*c.* 700–761 AD). It is a text that has challenged translators since the earliest attempt by W.J.B. Fletcher in 1919, for its complexity lies in its utter simplicity, a paradox that early Chinese poets played with in their writings.

Weinberger takes us through the poem step by step. Each version is set out on the left-hand page, with the editor's comment facing it starting with the Chinese, so that we can see the layout of the characters and learn that each one represents a word of a single syllable. This is followed by a transliteration of the poem, giving a sense of the sounds and rhyme scheme, then a character-by-character translation. It is at this point that we begin to grasp the enormity of the translator's task, for not only can characters be nouns, verbs or adjectives, they can also have contradictory meanings. Hence, a character in one line can be either [\i jing] (brightness) or [\i ying] (shadow). Moreover, there is no tense in Chinese verbs, and no differentiation between singular and plural.

All of which means that the translator has to make deliberate choices and justify them in the English version. This, of course, is what all translators do, but faced with a text such as this, and given a number of translators' attempts to create an English poem, the starkness of the translator's decision-making is laid bare for all to see.

The earliest English version uses a rhyme scheme popular in his time, but banal when we think about the kind of language Fletcher's contemporary, Ezra Pound, was using in his translations from the Chinese.

Here are the opening lines of Pounds' Poem by the Bridge at Ten-Shin:

> March has come to the bridge head.
> Peach boughs and apricot boughs hand over a thousand gates,
> At morning there are flowers to cut the heart,
> And evening drives them on the eastward-flowing waters.

Pound's imagist technique is apparent here, as he creates the mood that will colour the rest of the poem. Pound's translations are so good that they extended the boundaries of English poetry, offering native writers new opportunities. Fletcher's version of Wang Wei, in contrast, seems very

English and very dull, employing a four line rhyming pattern reminiscent of a greetings card:

> So lone seem the hills; there is no one in sight there.
> But whence is the echo of voices I hear?
> The rays of the sunset pierce slanting the forest,
> And in their reflection green mosses appear.

Weinberger accuses Fletcher of 'stuffing the original into the corset of traditional verse form' (Weinberger, 1987).

Certainly, we cannot grasp from this version as to why this poem should have occupied such an important place in Chinese literature and been considered so beautiful. The translator has failed to recreate the poem or, in Weinberger's terms, to 're-imagine' the poem. The key is to recognise the visual quality and for the translator to see the scene and transmit that vision to the reader.

Comparing the different versions, we can see how translators struggled to understand the pictorial aspect of the scene sketched by the Chinese poet. 'Slanting sunlight/Casts motley patterns on the jade-green mosses' is an image offered by Chang Yin-nan and Lewis C. Walmersley. 'The slanting such at evening penetrates the deep woods' is Soame Jenyns' offering, while G.W. Robinson writes two lines:

> With light coming back into the deep word
> The top of the green moss is lit again.

All these translators have produced versions of Wang Wei's image of sunlight in a forest, though with significant differences. Chang Yin-nan and Lewis stress the patterns of the sunlight in an almost psychedelic image, Jenyns has decided that it is evening and Robinson in contrast seems to be suggesting that the sunlight is returning.

Weinberger's assessment of the different versions is done with skill and erudition, and he insists on the importance of the visual. He points out that most translators of Chinese poetry are scholars, but they are not poets, while a few are good poets but have little Chinese. He singles out Kenneth Rexroth's version for praise, pointing out that it 'comes closest to the spirit, if not the letter, of the original', adding that Rexroth's version is what Wang Wei might have written had he been born a 20th century American. Using free verse, Rexroth renders the two lines as three:

> The low rays of the sun
> Slip through the dark forest,

And gleam again on the
Shadowy moss.

In terms of translation that makes the most impact, it is Gary Snyder's 1978 version that wins both my vote and Weinberger's. Snyder has created a modern American imagist poem about a flash of sunlight in the deep forest. Snyder understands mountains and forests, having direct experience of such landscapes. Did he, then, see what his Chinese predecessor saw centuries before him? I like to think he did, for though translation is about change, it is also about continuity. Here is Snyder's version of Wang Wei:

Empty mountains:
No-one to be seen.
Yet-hear-human
sounds and echoes.
Returning sunlight
enters the dark woods;
Again shining
On the green moss, above.

Weinberger was so puzzled by the final preposition 'above', that he wrote to Snyder for an explanation. Snyder replied pointing out that in deep forests, moss grows up high, on trees; so rather than imagining a shaft of sunlight coming down illuminating moss on stones on the ground, Wang Wei was imagining the light high up in the trees.

A good translator needs to be able to visualise a scene, particularly in a poem such as this. By comparing how different translators have rendered the scene, we can see some of the difficulties they encountered in the process of visualising, and admire some of the more creative solutions.

What this kind of exercise highlights is the need for translators to be fully in control of their material, to have knowledge that goes beyond the immediately linguistic and to think imaginatively.

By foregrounding the word 'above' at the end of the poem, Snyder makes the reader look upwards, both in his imaginary forest and in figurative terms, thereby hinting at a mystical dimension to the scene. It is an object lesson in how the power of a single word in English can mirror the power of a single Chinese character.

First published in *ITI Bulletin* July–August 2003.

Chapter 31
Where the Fun Comes In

We all would probably agree that translation is a serious profession, requiring all kinds of skills. Such skills involve linguistic competence, of course, but all sorts of other competences besides. Translators have to be able to write well, they have to be excellent readers in order to grasp fully the meaning of whatever they are translating, and they have to have a great deal of additional knowledge so that they can assist their readers where necessary. But what is often forgotten, when we emphasise the serious intellectual undertaking that is translation, is that translating can also be fun. Language is infinitely supple, and what translators can do, which monolinguals cannot, is to experiment with the plasticity of more than one language.

Many of us, old and young, enjoy reading *Asterix* comics. We enjoy the stories, the graphics and, above all, the puns and ridiculous names: Obelix, the strong man, Getafix, the village druid, chief Vitalstatistix, Cacophonix the bard. For some of us that enjoyment is heightened by the admiration we feel for the translators, Anthea Bell and Derek Hockridge, for translating comic books full of jokes and wordplay is a tough assignment. Yet, there are translators who revel in the opportunity to play with words: translators of Queneau, Apollinaire, Joyce, Roald Dahl and, one of the most frequently translated of all, Lewis Carroll, all engage in linguistic gamesmanship. In short, they all play with words and the ability to play is an essential part of translation.

Anthea Bell's father was Adrian Bell, one of the leading compilers of crossword puzzles for *The Times*. Growing up with a father who constantly played with language, she recalls how her father would test clues on his children at breakfast time. This anecdote is related in a beautiful little book, enigmatically titled *Pretty Girl with Crimson Rose*, by Sandy Balfour that came out in 2003. The subtitle is equally intriguing: *A Memoir of Love, Exile and Crosswords*. Yet, the subtitle is very apt, for the book is indeed a memoir of all three, and as he learns about crosswords, Balfour tells the story of his life as a South African emigré to London coming to terms with his uprootedness and continually having to rethink and reassess what has gone before. The book is very different from Eva Hoffman's *Lost in Translation*, yet takes up similar themes, albeit more playfully.

For play is the secret to solving crossword puzzles, which involves careful reading, decoding and a wide vocabulary, all skills that translators need to have too. The title clue is clarified in Chapter 6 (we put belle, which means pretty girl, inside red, which means crimson, and we get REBELLED, which means rose), but the focus of the chapter is Balfour's comment that 'like a crossword clue, history never quite makes sense at first reading. The surface is plausible, but discordant' (Balfour, 2003). Only after subsequent readings does history start to make sense, he argues, as he writes about a visit to East Berlin just before the Wall came down and about the release of Nelson Mandela a few months later in 1990.

Decoding, making sense and playing with language are essential to good translation. For some translators, working with writers who also played skilful language games is an additional challenge, and just as the crossword solver has to go through several stages of interpretation and understanding, so also does the translator of this kind of text. Edwin Morgan is a great translator, whose own poetry shows the delight he takes in stretching language – in his case both English and Scots – to extremes. Commenting on his translations of Eugenio Montale, Morgan astutely notes the subtlety with which the Italian poet manipulated ambiguity, rhyme, assonance, alliteration, rhythm and onomatopoeia, pointing out that these 'defy an exact point-to-point rendering' (Edwin Morgan, 1996: 5). Despite this admission, he declares that he has 'not avoided the attempt to take care of them, even if sometimes under the principle of "equivalence of effect"' (Morgan, 1996: 5).

Morgan's notes on his translations of the Russian poet Vladimir Mayakovsky are similarly sensitive and intelligent. He translated some of Mayakovsky into English, and then translated other poems into Scots. There is a vein of 'fantastic satire' in Scots poetry, he maintains, that goes back through Burns to the Scottish Renaissance and which 'seems to accommodate Mayakovsky more readily than anything in English verse' (Morgan, 1996: 113). He argues that by identifying a Scots tradition of poetry that is closer to Russian than anything English, he is better able to translate the game-playing, unorthodox, irreverent Russian, hence the choice of Scots rather than Standard English.

And then Morgan adds that he also chose to work in Scots because 'there was an element of challenge' in trying to see whether the language could match 'the racy colloquialism and verbal inventiveness in Mayakovsky's Russian' (Morgan, 1996: 113). Translating a writer who stretched his own language to previously undreamed of limits, Morgan seeks to push the boundaries of Scots, tapping into a traditional seam of poetry and at the same time experimenting with the language that has evolved.

Morgan is an example of a translator who is also a poet and someone with an encyclopaedic knowledge of literature, but what makes his translations good is his ability to experiment and to play, which is what makes the Bell–Hockridge translations so successful. Nor is this ability so exceptional: Sandy Balfour suggests that large number of people have great linguistic skills that they bring to the solving of crosswords. It would be interesting to know how many translators are also crossword addicts; I have to confess to being one myself.

Colette Rossant plays with language too, rather differently. She has written two books, described as 'memoirs with recipes', *Apricots on the Nile* (2004) and *Return to Paris* (2003). The books tell the story of an uneasy childhood and adolescence, as the Franco-Egyptian girl leaves the Cairo she comes to love in childhood and her adoring Egyptian grandparents for the troubled world of post-war Paris, from which she eventually escapes with her American husband. Just as the crossword puzzles provide the thread that connects the places to which Sandy Balfour travels and the discoveries he makes about himself and the world he lives in, so in Colette Rossant's books the thread is supplied by recipes. The books therefore have a dual purpose: they can be read for the pleasure they provide, and they can also be used in the kitchen. Rossant's recipe for avgolemono soup is just one of the dishes that can be strongly recommended.

Rossant gives the reader the recipes not as clues to a mystery but as a means of understanding her history of cultural displacement. She does not shy away from using French and Arabic terms and provides straightforward English translations in brackets on first use. So, for example, the first time we encounter the word *semit* it is explained as the Egyptian version of a soft pretzel, and the English for *ful medamas* (braised brown fava beans) is also provided, but thereafter the words are used in the expectation that the reader will have learned their meaning. This, of course, parallels what happens in cooking: the aspirant cook has to learn a new terminology and then start to use it.

The phenomenon of the intercultural memoir that plays with language is new, as is the way in which translation is employed in such works. Sandy Balfour even gives us a joke in Afrikaans, followed straight away by the English version, but elsewhere the odd Afrikaans word is left untranslated. This way of writing deliberately involves the reader in a level of playfulness also, for we have no choice but to reflect on the strangeness of words that we cannot understand, and imagine what they might mean if no translation were provided. If the words are translated, then like the translator we are given the opportunity to see two parallel worlds and made aware of the fact that there is more than one way of saying something.

In his useful handbook for translators, Clifford Landers (2001) states that there is no aspect of translation more frustrating and yet at the same time potentially more rewarding than metalanguage. 'Nowhere do the joys and travails of translation coexist as visibly as in the close combat between a translator and a play of words,' he writes, playing himself with the idea of a battle between the translator and the work. Landers believes that the ability to play with words and in particular to transfer puns and jokes across languages requires an ability on the part of the translator to think outside the box. Sandy Balfour would doubtless say the same thing about crossword puzzle solvers, and as we are forced by the task in hand, whether to translate, to solve a puzzle or to describe how to create a dish, to be creative with language and to be playful, we acquire new ways of seeing the world.

First published in *ITI Bulletin* November–December 2004.

Chapter 32
Translators Making the News

For the past few months, I have been working with the research team setting up a three-year project that will investigate the politics and economics of translation in global media. The project has been funded by the Arts and Humanities Research Board, and it is very exciting to be involved with this kind of interdisciplinary, trans-cultural research.

The idea behind the project is that translation plays a huge role in the global circulation of news, but amazingly, we know very little about how that role operates. How translators are selected is one interesting question, whether they arrive somehow at translating news reports, or whether they intend to be news translators from the outset. This raises the equally interesting question of training, and whether such translators are trained or whether they learn on the job.

Anecdotal evidence so far suggests that there is no systematic training at all. I have an anecdote of my own to add to these stories. Many years ago, I stood in as a holiday replacement for a friend who had a regular news-reading slot very late at night on a world service broadcasting channel. I had no training whatsoever (nor had she), and the job consisted of arriving in the studio at about 1 am, collecting a pile of papers in one language, doing a rough translation, then shaping the material to fit a 10-minute slot allocated for reading the news and going on air to deliver it two hours later. The job was therefore to translate, edit, rewrite and read a news bulletin constructed out of a bundle of miscellaneous documents of unknown origin. This could be seen as the translation equivalent of the sheep-to-suit race; when a sheep is sheared, the wool is carded, spun, woven into cloth, cut and sewn and finally worn. I believe the world record is less than 24 hours for the whole process. That late night news job was not dissimilar.

How much have things changed since those bad old days? Apparently not a great deal, if our preliminary research is to be believed. Despite the hugely significant role of translation in our increasingly globalised world, translator training is patchy and in the news environment, there are other complicating factors. For a start, there are time constraints. This was always the case, but today, with 24-hour breaking news channels on TV worldwide and the endless up-to-the-second information that circulates on the internet, news has to travel faster than ever before. It also has to be more reliable, in that today's audiences have higher expectations of accuracy and honesty in news reporting than previous generations did. Of course, this is not to suggest that journalists years ago were less honest and reliable than journalists today, nor that readers of newspapers were more gullible, merely that with the supply of sources that enable double-checking of information all around us, journalists have to take more care to ensure the veracity of their news items, yet they have less time in which to do this. The international furore over still unproven claims about weapons of mass destruction in Iraq, and the recent scandal of the British newspaper that published hoax photographs of prisoners being abused, a hoax that led to the dismissal of the editor, serve as examples of how demanding the public now is where truthful reporting is concerned. We want facts, and we want to know that those facts are genuine, but from the journalists' point of view, the time constraints in ensuring reliability are increasing the pressure on their work all the time.

Besides investigating how translators come to be working in media translation and exploring their working conditions and relationships within the world of journalism and television news reporting, another area that we hope to study is how translation affects meaning as it circulates through global news.

Everyone knows the old truism about one person's terrorist being another person's freedom fighter, and this principle can be applied much more widely where news reporting is concerned. Not only are styles of writing and presentation completely different in different cultures, but so also are the conventions that govern what can and cannot be said. Such conventions range from overt censorship, where journalists are simply not allowed to say certain things for fear of arrest and imprisonment to other forms of constraint. Libel laws are particularly powerful in the United Kingdom, for example, while elsewhere respect for social practices may make the public discussion of certain items in the media unacceptable. In transferring news across cultures, social, legal and linguistic conventions can radically alter what is reported and how it is presented. One way of investigating these differences, which can result in shifts of emphasis and meaning, is through comparative case studies, whereby the same event or issue as reported in the media in different languages is explored in depth.

In the spring of 2004, we held a one-day seminar at the University of Warwick to initiate the project. The main objective was to bring together translators, people studying translation and journalists, for the success of the project depends on being able to bridge the gap that (sadly) often yawns between academics and practitioners. On that occasion, the barriers were well and truly broken down, and the success of the experiment could be seen by the number of people still wanting to ask questions even after sitting in a hot room for hours on one of the sunniest days of the year.

Among the speakers who kindly agreed to come and share their experience of working in the field of international news reporting were leading figures from Reuters, Agence France Presse and the Inter Press Service, along with specialist scholars from Finland and Ireland, the editor of an exciting new journal *Global Media and Communication*, and an experienced translator of financial and business news.

Some of the memorable phrases I noted down include: 'We can't get away from translation in news agencies,' 'Millions of words are rushing round the world every hour of every day,' 'Translation shows up the extent of the cultural problems we face,' 'Translation is never just a question of translating words' and 'Translation is a critical path through the world not just a route round the margins.'

We heard about the difficult choice that translators have to make, about the fundamental problem of moving from the global to the local, then back from the local to the global, all the time endeavouring not to offend anyone, about the attempts to use non-inflammatory, neutral language that will enable people not involved in a situation to make up their own minds.

We heard about specific writing problems that translators have to contend with, such as English under-statement, the use of the conditional tense in French, the importance of opening statements in some languages or the need for a powerful concluding statement in others, all of which involve complex processes of rewriting in order to comply with the expectations of the designated readership or audience.

Readers in some cultures, we learned, expect news reports to contain direct speech in inverted commas, whereas others would never expect direct quotes and want reported speech instead. Knowing the conventions of reporting in different languages is clearly a crucial skill.

Underpinning the project is the serious question we posed when first deciding to take this task on board: why, given the fundamental importance of translation in the worldwide dissemination of news, are translators invisible?

It is hoped that by highlighting the role played by translators, and by investigating not only how those translators work but also what other factors are involved in the business of transferring information, we can help to raise the profile of translation and remind monolingual readers and audiences that the world is buzzing with different languages and different ways of thinking.

First published in the *ITI Bulletin* July–August 2004.

Chapter 33
What Exactly Did Saddam Say?

In our world of mass communication, of ever-increasing speed, our world of 24-hour breaking news, where text messages can be sent from scenes of disaster even as politicians are issuing statements denying that the disaster has happened, the one certain thing that we all cling to is the importance of the truthfulness of news reporters. We need to believe in the veracity of the accounts provided by those men and women around the world who supply us with information about the events that shape our lives. When such information is proven to be false, we are outraged. In 2004, the editor of a national British newspaper was forced to resign when he authorised the publication of photographs, purporting to show British soldiers abusing prisoners in Iraq that turned out to be fakes. In such a situation, we all feel abused. In those countries where governments interfere with the freedom of the press, we are equally outraged, for press freedom and truthfulness go hand in hand.

In 2003, I began directing a research project at the University of Warwick, funded by the Arts and Humanities Research Board that investigated the role of translation in the production of international news. Our project was entitled 'The Politics and Economics of Translation in Global Media', and what we sought to do was to explore how translation functions in the transfer of news across linguistic and cultural boundaries. We have been working with translators, news reporters and senior figures in international news agencies as well as academics, for without the input of practitioners, the research would be pointless. What we have learned so far is very interesting, and yet at the same time it is paradoxical. For on the one hand, it is clear that translation plays a fundamental role in the transfer of news around the world, an increasingly prominent role in an age that demands constant global coverage, and yet on the other hand it is also clear that very different definitions of translation are being used, and very different translation conventions are operating.

Pragmatically speaking, it is obvious that items written in one language cannot be translated line by line into another. It would take far too long, and would probably be unnecessary. What is needed is more often a translation that is at the same time a synthesis of the original, so that in the translation process the reporter summarises and makes the necessary stylistic adjustments to ensure that the final product will meet the expectations of readers. Recently, reading the papers in Italy and listening to the news bulletins, I was reminded yet again of the different conventions operating in English and in Italian, the former tending towards understatement and often making use of irony, the latter preferring a more heightened language and more consciously crafted rhetoric. French newspaper readers like to follow a story through to its denouement, while English readers like to have the facts of the case set down in the first paragraph (or even in the headline) and then follow an account of how that case came into being. Everything, from the length of sentences to the use of punctuation is conventionalised, and different papers have their own house style as well.

Information passing between cultures via news agencies is therefore reshaped, edited, synthesised and yet this process is also referred to as translation. At the same time, many journalists also talk about 'translators' or 'pure translation', by which they appear to indicate what might be referred to by others as 'literal translation', though most translators would seriously question such a definition. It would seem from our preliminary investigations that in the global media world, the boundaries of the definition of translation have been recast, and that the concept of translation which linguists and language teachers might hold to is very different from the one that is in use in international news reporting.

The question of both definitions of translation and the veracity of translated accounts was particularly apparent in the reporting of the first course appearance of Saddam Hussein in July 2004. Not all the British papers carried transcripts of the relatively brief appearance of the former Iraqi dictator before a judge, but those that did published texts that were surprisingly different. The transcript published in *The Independent* carried a health warning:

> The following is an edited transcript of the translators' words as Saddam Hussein answered questions from the judge Ra'id Juhi. Some parts of the conversation were not included in the original transcript.

What I think is being stated here is that during the hearing translators were producing their version of what was being said and that when it was over, the translators' text was compared with the official transcript that did not contain all the parts of the conversation translated by the translators. However, I do not know that and can only surmise.

The Daily Telegraph published what was described as a 'transcript', but added a prefatory sentence stating: 'Saddam's courtroom exchanges with the judge yesterday included', which was then followed by a shorter version than that published in *The Independent*.

To what extent do these two transcripts differ from one another, was the question I posed, along with a connected question about trust and veracity. For since I have no Arabic, I needs must trust what I read in English as offering an accurate, truthful version of what took place in the courtroom. Like other readers in a similar situation, I am dependent on the translator to provide an authentic, impartial record of what took place. So how can I assess the veracity of the following exchange:

The Independent, 2 July 2004:

The judge opened proceedings by asking Saddam for his name:

Saddam: Hussein Majid, the president of the Republic of Iraq.

The judge then asks his date of birth.

Saddam: 1937
Judge: Profession? Former president of the Republic of Iraq?
Saddam: No, present. Current. It's the will of the people.
Judge: The head of the Baath Party that is dissolved, defunct. Former commander and chief of the army. Residence is Iraq. Your mother's name?
Saddam: Sobha. You also have to introduce yourself to me.
Judge: Mr Saddam, I am the investigative judge of the central court of Iraq.
Saddam: So that I have to know, you are an investigative judge of the central court of Iraq? What resolution, what law formed this court.

The judge's response could not be heard.

The Daily Telegraph, 2 July 2004:

Judge: Are you the former president of Iraq?
Saddam: I am Saddam Hussein, president of Iraq.
Judge: (to court clerk): Put down 'former' in brackets.
Saddam: I am the president of the republic so you should not strip me of my title to put me on trial.
Judge: You are the ex-leader of Iraq and the ex-leader of the dissolved armed forces. Were you the leader of the Ba'ath party and head of the armed forces?

Saddam:	Yes. I've introduced myself to you but you haven't introduced yourself to me. So who are you?
Judge:	I am a judge of the criminal courts of Iraq.
Saddam:	So you repress Iraqis under the orders of the coalition? Do you represent the American coalition?

Both these versions have been edited, as is clearly stated, but what is surprising is how different they are, in terms of information supplied, the structure of the questioning and responses, the choreography of the event (in one version we are told that the judge's reply cannot be heard, while the other version has the judge giving an instruction to the court clerk) and the tone. The judge in the first version comes across as a more authoritative figure. When he refers to Saddam's role as former chief of the army, he states this rather than putting it as a question which is the case in the second version. He also asks for the name of Saddam's mother, which is not recorded in *The Daily Telegraph*. The judge answers Saddam's question quite differently in each version: he claims to be variously the 'investigative judge of the central court of Iraq' and 'a judge of the criminal courts of Iraq'.

The differences between the two versions become more notable as we read on. Saddam makes much longer speeches in *The Independent* and challenges the judge on several occasions. The charges are listed, which is not the case in *The Daily Telegraph*. The concluding exchange is also rather different. In *The Independent*, Saddam refuses to sign any documents without his lawyers and the hearing ends with a robust exchange between the two parties:

Saddam:	Please allow me not to sign anything until the lawyers are present.
Judge:	That is fine. But this is your ...
Saddam:	I speak for myself.
Judge:	Yes, as a citizen you have the right. But the guarantees you have to sign because these were read to you, recited to you.
Saddam:	Anyway, why are you worried? I will come again before you with the presence of the lawyers, and you will be giving me all of these documents again. So why should we rush any action now and make mistakes because of rushed and hasty decisions or actions?
Judge:	No, this is not a hasty decision-making now. I'm just investigating. And we need to conclude and seal the minutes.
Saddam:	No, I will sign when the lawyers are present.

Judge:	Then you can leave.
Saddam:	Finished?
Judge:	Yes.

In *The Daily Telegraph* the hearing ends differently:

Saddam:	Would you accept if I do not sign this until the attendance of my lawyers?
Judge:	This is one of your rights.
Saddam:	I am not interfering with your responsibilities.
Judge:	Fine, then let it be recorded that he has not signed. You are dismissed from the court.
Saddam:	Finished?
Judge:	Finished.
Saddam:	(as he is led away by guards): Take it easy, I'm an old man.

Here there is no altercation, Saddam says very little before he is dismissed by the judge and a remark he apparently made to his guards is recorded as his final comment.

Do these details matter? Surely, one might ask, there is no need to nitpick over a text in this way when both versions effectively give us the gist of what happened in the Iraqi court. But from the perspective of a translation analyst, these differences matter greatly, for the two texts create a very different impression of the event and, were they to be dramatised, actors would find themselves playing very different roles depending on which script they were given. *The Independent* version has some awkward turns of phrase that suggest translationese and on the whole this version sounds slightly more foreign than the other. It is also much longer. The text in *The Daily Telegraph* has been domesticated and includes what can only be described as stage directions. The Saddam in this version is not so much an obstreperous former dictator on the defensive, but a somewhat ridiculous figure, in contrast with the restrained urbanity of the judge who uses language that might be heard in an English court. These subtle textual differences lead readers in slightly different directions.

Returning to our starting point, however, the question remains as to whether either of these texts is a truthful account of the hearing. Both are edited, and the longer version admits that parts of the conversation were not included in the original transcript, though gives no indication of where those additions might have come from. We are left with a sense of uneasiness: if we have no Arabic, then we cannot check the accuracy or otherwise of these versions against any published transcript in the source language. But in any case, what we have here are two English translations of a transcript of a court hearing that took place in Arabic, both of which have been edited in different ways. We could say that whole series of different processes of translation have taken place: from spoken to written, from Arabic to English, from full length to abbreviated, from initial copy to in-house style tailored for a particular readership. At every stage of those different processes, manipulations have taken place, although we are still invited to accept that the final product is a true and accurate version for English readers.

First published in *The Linguist* 43 (6), 2004.

Chapter 34
Native Strengths

There appears to be a crisis in language learning in England right now. Foreign language teaching in state schools has declined rapidly since the government decided to abolish compulsory language study after the age of 14, university language departments are increasingly in crisis as numbers dwindle. What exacerbates the situation though is the complacency of people who argue that this does not matter because after all, what the world wants is people who speak English. Those lucky enough to be born native speakers of English do not need to bother learning any other language. English is the language of business, of international communication and of the globalised 21st century.

Personally, I deplore this attitude, and the other day I found myself speaking rather sharply to someone who was complaining about a niece at school in Wales who is being made to learn Welsh as part of the curriculum. A complete waste of time, this person was saying, why force children to learn a language that is not going to be of any use to anyone when they could be improving their English. He went on to add that Welsh would be extinct by the end of the century anyway, whereas the whole world by then would be speaking English.

Now Welsh happens to be one of the languages I would most like to learn, along with Russian and Japanese, because I have some sense of the extraordinary richness of Welsh literature and because I love the sound of the spoken language, and so I suppose I was provoked somewhat by this man's (to me) ignorance. For the point of learning Welsh in a Welsh school is that language carries with it a sense of cultural heritage, and in a world of Macdonaldisation preserving one's cultural heritage and with it establishing a sense of cultural identity has never been so important. True, millions of people are learning English in order to pursue international careers, but they proudly maintain their own languages alongside it. It could be argued that the diffusion of English is simultaneously serving to make people more aware of their own particular linguistic heritage, as it has often been pointed out that the counter-face of globalisation is localisation.

Trying to argue against the teaching of Welsh in Welsh schools is particularly ironic, for the endurance of the Celtic languages of the British Isles is clear evidence of the potential of languages spoken by a minority population to survive in the face of all odds. Speakers of Welsh, Gaelic and Irish have struggled for centuries against the dominance of English, a dominance that has at times been imposed by force. The persecution of bards, carriers of the lore and literature of Ireland is well known, the Highland clearances were accompanied by an anti-Gaelic policy, the speaking of Celtic languages in schools was frequently punished and the status of the languages derided. Brian Friel's hugely successful play, *Translations*, tackles the subject of the ban on Irish and the deliberate policy of renaming places in an attempt to excise traces of the native language from the very landscape. Yet despite this dismal history, the languages have survived. True, Cornish and Manx faded and died out as the population of those regions declined, but what we have seen in the twentieth century has been a revival of interest in the Celtic languages, assisted now by the EU policy that seeks to preserve minority languages. The Irish Literary Revival of the late 19th–early 20th century was followed by the Scottish Renaissance in the 1920s, when both Scots and Gaelic reemerged as languages with significant literary status. Today, English may be the world's most dominant language, but it coexists in the British Isles with three of the languages that successive governments over centuries were unable to eliminate, and with Scots effectively now seen as a fourth language rather than as a dialect of English.

Translation has played a role in the preservation and development of these languages. In the 16th century, the translation of The Bible into Welsh had as great an impact on the Welsh language as the 1611 Authorised Version of The Bible had on English. Translation has provided new literary models, and more recently technical and bureaucratic translation has expanded the lexical and syntactical range. As has often been argued, translation frequently plays a major role in strengthening cultures that find themselves in a marginal position. But there is also an aspect to translation that should not be ignored; as Michael Cronin (2006a) has pointed out in his book, *Translation and Globalization*, there is an unequal power relationship between minority and majority languages, and hence translation tends to be unidirectional, with the language perceived as least powerful absorbing most from the dominant language which often remains impervious to the other. Speakers of minority languages such as Irish need translation, he says, in order to be able to enjoy the same rights as English language speakers, and certainly because Irish is an official language of the European Community, all documents have to be translated into it.

However, there is a danger of linguistic interference, as the language in the less powerful position is compelled to adjust to input from the dominant partner. Traditionally, languages have reacted differently to importation: English has tended to absorb and welcome loan words, while French, for example, has resisted. The position of a minority language is a more delicate one, for the very act of translation is an attempt both to preserve and to strengthen, not to dilute it.

Cronin also points out that translation theorists have tended to ignore minority language issues so far. He is right, of course, to draw our attention to the ambiguous role played by translation and to point out that this ambiguity has not received the scholarly attention it deserves. On the one hand, the survival of the Celtic languages has been assisted by translation, while on the other hand, the very fact that translation happens in such an unequal way means that those languages are importing much more than they export, and still remain invisible to the majority population of these islands. This is a dilemma that will be immediately recognisable to anyone using a minority language anywhere in the world.

On balance, though, I believe that translation has had a predominantly positive effect, and the survival of the Celtic languages is clear evidence for this. The importance of a public bilingual strategy is also significant. As we see place names in two languages, and read road signs and other notices in two languages so, on some level we absorb some degree of awareness of difference. Just recognising that there can be two names for the same town or village shows us that there is more than one way of looking at the same thing. The great danger for monolinguals is lack of that kind of awareness, a failure to recognise that other cultures are other, and that linguistic diversity is not just a freak of history, but is part of the way in which different societies articulate themselves. It fascinates me, for example, that English and Welsh do not share a terminology for the same colour spectrum, since English has four words to distinguish between grey, green, blue and brown and Welsh has three, despite the geography, the landscape and the light being virtually identical. How have such differences emerged and why, and does this mean that what we see is fundamentally different?

Recognising difference is a first step to understanding otherness, so as to learn to live with it and accommodate different behaviours and different sets of values. This, rather than any other reason, is why it is important for children to learn another language. The objective of language teaching should not be so much to enable children to buy a train ticket in another country, where in all probability English will be spoken, but rather to begin to understand that what can be said in one language cannot always be said in another, that each language has its own special features and that translation therefore involves negotiation and compromise.

Research also suggests that children who acquire a second language early have a facility for further language acquisition. I was at the University of Limerick recently, talking to students who studied English and Irish at school and have moved on to Spanish, French and Japanese in a trilingual undergraduate programme. Students in India are often able to move comfortably between four or five languages, as are so many people in an increasingly multilingual Europe.

The survival of minority languages is vital to all our futures, and the best way to ensure that survival is to keep teaching those languages to the next generation wherever possible, and to ensure that all children are able to learn some other language at some point in their lives. And let us not forget that though the dominance of English may be a fact right now, but by the end of this century Mandarin could be the next lingua franca.

First published in *ITI Bulletin* July–August 2006.

Chapter 35
What's in a Name?

I have always enjoyed airports, watching people arrive and depart and looking up at boards telling you where the next flights are going. These days, though, I find myself questioning my geographical knowledge, for frequently there are place names that I have never seen before. Musing on what appears to be an increasing number of new places, I came to the conclusion that this trend reflects the changes of today's world where more and more people previously unable to obtain passports can travel freely and tiny airports in what were once remote places grow in size and importance. There have been regular flights from Birmingham to Kazakhstan now for years, once the new Asian republics gained their independence from the Soviet Union.

But besides the increased number of places now appearing on airport lists, there is another significant change afoot: the renaming of places, the return, if you like, to more local nomenclature and away from names that had become internationalised through decades of colonial commerce. Peking is now known globally as Beijing, a relatively slight but significant change, less obvious perhaps than Madras becoming Chennai or Bombay being known as Mumbai. The re-Africanisation of place names is something we have all become accustomed to, with former Rhodesia now Zimbabwe, Nyasaland now Malawi, French Sudan now Mali, but the changes to orthography and pronunciation of names in the Indian subcontinent and South-East Asia is a more recent phenomenon. Nor are changes of name always straightforward. The regime in Burma, for example, set up a commission to find a new name for the state and came up with Myanmar in 1989. The name of Burma had been adopted by the English in the 18th century from the Portuguese, who in turn had derived it from the more local Bama. However, opponents of the military regime, including the Nobel peace prize winner Aung San Sun Kyi opposed the name change on the grounds that it was based on a spurious idea of national inclusiveness and effectively marginalised part of the population. International uneasiness with the new name remains, even though it has been adopted by the United Nations.

What such changes illustrate is the immense political significance of place names. In a post-colonial world, the old system of nomenclature needs to change. When I was a child in the 1950s, the process of moving on from the stage of European colonisation was proceeding, often violently, along. In those days without television and 24-hour breaking news, we knew next to nothing about what was going on around the world, and a popular hobby was collecting stamps from exotic places in other continents with English or French names, names that now exist only in philatelists' albums. I do not think it occurred to me or my peers to question why English names featured so prominently on the map, though I do remember being puzzled when told that parts of South America were 'still unknown'. Surely, the people who live there know about them, I mused, but clearly that was not the point being made. It took a while longer before I understood the implications of that notion of unknowing.

Independence involves an assertion of independent identity, and renaming plays a vital role. For renaming has also been important in suppressing identity and, as Brian Friel has shown so brilliantly in his play about Irish place names, aptly titled *Translations* denying the people the right to name their places in their own language is one of the most primitive, yet most powerful instruments of oppression. The insistence of Celtic-speaking peoples on bilingual place name signs, for example, is not, as someone once said to me, just an affection; it is an assertion of the right of people to use their own language and name the world through that language as they choose and as their ancestors chose also.

A few years ago I was invited to Katowice in Poland, one of those places that now appears on airport boards all over the United Kingdom as more and more Poles travel to Britain for work. I was unsure quite where it was located, so got out my old school atlas (I confess, pathetically, to using an atlas from the *scuola media* from half a century ago!) only to find that it did not exist. I hunted and hunted, then rang a friend who I thought might be better informed. Katowice used to be known as Katowitz, I was told, but there was nothing like that name either. All I could find in the place where the city ought to have been was somewhere called *Stalinograd*. Yes, said my Polish friends, when I told them about my search, that is what it was, just as St Petersburg was Leningrad for some considerable time. Today, every trace of the old Soviet dictator has gone from Katowice, starting with the name reversal.

Dictators have had a penchant to have places named after them. Poor Pontivy in Brittany was twice renamed Napoleonville, Sadr City in Baghdad was once Saddam City and Porfirio Diaz has left his name all over Mexico. Bolivia, of course, is named after Simon Bolivar, judged rather more kindly by history than some of the above names. Queen Victoria's name resounds around the former empire, from the Victoria Falls to the state of Victoria. Perhaps even more places are named after navigators, with the classic example being the obscure Amerigo Vespucci after whom two continents have been named.

Naming places after people was, in the distant past, a handy way of identifying sites. Coventry may well derive its name from someone known as Cofa whose tree was a particular feature in the forest of Arden, while Fillongley, a village near to where I live was apparently named after the woodland clearing of the family or followers of someone named Fygla. The origin of many English place names is a combination of topographical features with the names of individuals associated with them, though with the passing of time the original meaning has disappeared.

The names given to the same places in different languages are also a rich source of meaning and can shed light on historical differences. English maintains that the English Channel divides the British Isles from the rest of Europe, while for the French it is la Manche, a sleeve of water with no national associations, though interestingly, the Channel Islands in French become the Isles Anglo-Normandes. The North Sea was once claimed as the German Ocean, and Poland has seen a bewildering number of name changes as Russian and German regimes laid claim to Polish territory. On the other side of the world, the island known more generally as Borneo is Kalimantan to Indonesians, while Malaysians refer to the Northern area as East Malaysia, since it has sovereignty over that region. Borneo in fact comprises three distinct states, with the Sultanate of Brunei the smallest, and wealthiest.

Fascinating also is the question of when and why some place names are translated while others are not. Venezia is Venice, with the stress on the first syllable in English, Venice with the stress on the second syllable in French, and Venedig in German, though Verona is the same in all European languages. Similarly, Firenze becomes Florence in English and French, Florenz in German, Napoli is Naples and Neapol. These different versions of extremely well-known places reflect the importance attributed to them in previous times and the desire on the part of other nations to assert some kind of stake in those cities, a desire that undoubtedly grew during the age of the Grand Tour and the emergence of tourism.

In some cases, the translation may involve a slight shift of spelling that ensures that the place name fits into the rhythmic pattern of the translating languages, as is the case of the Englishing of Genova or Padova to Genoa and Padua, but at other times it may involve much more. Livorno was Leghorn in English during the period when it was a major port, and today both names are in use in standard English, a point I started to note a few years ago and puzzle over. The conclusion I came to is that reverting to the Italian Livorno over Leghorn is not a political statement, but rather a sign of greater familiarity with the Italian language through greater contact in different ways, but it continues to intrigue.

The prominence of certain places at different times has undoubtedly led to some names being translated. Such places may be capital cities, ports, commercial centres, seas, rivers or even mountains. The Thames, for example, is the Italian Tamigi, while the Roman Tevere is the English Tiber. Besides the political dimension of naming, there is also an important commercial history, and the story of how places rise and fall in significance for different cultures at different times is often fascinating. What is important to remember, however, is that naming and renaming is not an innocent act, it happens because power is asserted in some way, sometimes as an act of liberation but also, regrettably, as an act of oppression or cultural appropriation. Understanding why place names change is another way of understanding the world in which we move.

First published in *ITI Bulletin* July–August 2007.

Chapter 36
Food for Thought

The other day, in a restaurant in Lisbon, I ordered what I thought was swordfish, *peixe espada* – a slender, white piece of fish materialised, delicious but certainly not the hard dark flesh of swordfish. My Portuguese friends were equally mystified, until we looked again at the menu. The English version of the menu said 'scabbard fish', which we had simply assumed to be an inadequate rendering of swordfish. We were inclined to be snooty about the quality of the translated menu, for everyone has encountered ludicrously badly translated menus that provide endless entertainment. However, comparing the translation with the original clarified everything in this case, though my friends admitted they had never heard of a scabbard fish either. What they did admit was that the usual Portuguese term for swordfish is *espadarte*, though in Spanish it is *pez espada*, which is where our linguistic confusion occurred. The Spanish for scabbard fish is *pez cinto*.

I now know quite a bit about scabbard fish, whose Latin name is *Lepidopus caudatus*. It is a long silvery fish and does look vaguely like a scabbard for a dagger. It is apparently found around the world but principally in the western Mediterranean off the southern coast of Portugal, Madeira and the Azores. There is a black variety that is often served in Madeiran restaurants. But since it never turns up on the menus of Northern European, and its name in Portuguese so closely approximates to the Spanish for swordfish, it is perhaps not surprising that I ordered the wrong meal. The translator of the menu, however, was absolutely correct. *Peixe espada* is indeed a scabbard fish.

Translating the names of local flora and fauna is notoriously difficult. Fish names seem to me to be particularly hard, partly because so many fish have local names because they are particular to certain places, and partly also because often the same fish is labelled differently on account of different cooking and eating habits. Fortunately for translators today, there are wonderful multilingual data bases for flora and fauna now available on the internet, huge dictionaries of specialist terms. One of my favourites is the Multilingual Multiscript Plant Name Database, which is enormous and endlessly fascinating. But despite these marvellous translation aids, there remains a basic problem around the translation of food, and this is linked to one of the most fundamental issues of interlingual communication generally. Food is so crucial in a society, and translating terms for food can often pose insurmountable problems to the translator. Even where an equivalent appears to exist, the food itself and the ways in which that food is eaten may vary enormously. So we have words in English for rice, and for bread, both food staples, but what the English person might envisage when they hear those words is completely different from what a Chinese person or a Frenchman might envisage. There are dozens of different varieties of rice and bread in China and France, and terminology to reflect differences. In English, we have rice and bread as catch-all words, words that categorise generally rather than defining more specifically and locally.

Cooking and eating practices, as anthropologists have always known, are culture bound. What is eaten, how it is cooked, indeed if it is cooked at all, how it is served and the ensuing rituals of eating vary enormously across cultures. The space for misunderstanding in this area is vast, and the degree to which any of us is able to adjust varies without experience. The exquisite beauty and elegance of a Japanese meal, where the colour, shape and material of every bowl in which food is served has been carefully chosen to accord with that food is always marred, for me, as an awkward Westerner, with the physical discomfort of sitting on the floor for hours. When I was in Central Asia, my hosts were delighted with me at first because I took lessons from them on how to eat pilau with one hand from a communal bowl, something some Westerners find revolting. However, my nemesis came when reprimanded for 'insulting the bread', that is, for putting it face down on the table, something that never even crossed my mind as having any meaning at all. European friends have often remarked on the slight uneasiness they experience when dining in Britain where there is no greeting similar to *Bon appetit* that starts off the meal with a convivial sense of shared good will.

In our increasingly globalised world, it is heartening to see how strong the traditions around food remain in many countries. There are ceremonial foods that have been eaten for centuries that are still served on special occasions, and rituals around cooking and eating that endure. My mother still invites grandchildren to stir the Christmas pudding mixture and make a wish, a Czech friend still arrives with jars of pickled vegetables as an end of summer gift, and *panettone* hangs from the ceiling in every grocer's shop in Italy as Christmas approaches.

Yet at the same time, there is an increasing internationalisation of food. The kiwi fruit, unknown in Europe when I was a child, is now on menus everywhere. Great jars of kiwi fruit in liqueur can be found in the Ka De We in Berlin at this time of year, and mango sorbet has found its way into small Sicilian ice-cream parlours. In Britain, the internationalisation of food has been perhaps more rapid and more extreme than elsewhere in Europe: pizza, various forms of pasta, balti, chicken tikka masala, scampi, moussaka and countless other dishes that only a few years ago would have been viewed as exotic are now served routinely in pubs and cafes and school cafeterias.

The unfamiliar is a source of anxiety to most of us, and unfamiliar food is especially problematic. The recent book by Tom Parker-Bowles on food that he has encountered in other parts of the world that would strike horror into conservative British breasts has aroused media interest. We are repelled and fascinated by the wichetty grub and the deep-fried locust, though we will tuck in to mussels and deep-fried prawns without turning a hair. I eat veal and suckling pig, but I flatly refused kitten once in Guangzhou, and though I enjoy kidneys in white wine sauce, I could not swallow a dish on intestines served once in Indonesia.

When I was a little girl and we lived in Denmark, my mother had a cookery book that I have kept. The author is listed simply as 'Susanne', and its title is unpretentiously *Danish Cookery*. Susanne's introduction is short and straightforward and addresses the issue of cultural boundaries head-on. 'Some of the dishes in this little book might seem so strange that you simply cannot muster up sufficient courage to try them out,' she writes, adding matter-of-factly, 'and nothing can be done about that of course'. She adds that probably Chinese cookery books have a recipe for swallow nests, 'and how do you feel about swallow nests, if you are frank?' Acknowledging prejudice from the outset, the book is clearly laid out, simply written and has some excellent recipes indeed.

My favourite Chinese cookery book does not have any recipes for any kind of birds' nests, but it does have some ingenious translations of ingredients. Jim Lee, the Chinese American cook recognised that compromises had to be made with ingredients only available locally, so has structured his recipes around the possibility of substitution. If Chinese preserved cucumber cannot be found, Jim advises using shredded sweet gherkins. His book is written for non-Chinese readers and in consequence is one of the most useful introductions to Chinese cuisine that I have come across.

The diverse cooking and eating practices in different societies give the traveller immediate insight into cultural differences. The translator then has the tough task of trying to bridge the inevitable expectation gap, effectively confronting untranslatability. The translator who had properly rendered *peixe espada* as scabbard fish was quite correct and it was not his/her fault that the fish might be unfamiliar to foreigners. Perhaps the best way of engaging with another culture is through sharing food, through trying strange new dishes and observing different customs, effectively translating experientially.

First published in *ITI Bulletin* January–February 2007.

Chapter 37
Family Matters

Over the past 50 years, there have been some radical changes in family structures in the Western world. Back in the 1950s, divorce was spoken of in hushed tones, but today the odds on a newlywed couple divorcing at least once in their lives are pretty high. And with divorces come other changes: children by different marriages, with different sets of grandparents, aunts and uncles. One friend of mine talks cheerfully about his three sets of in-laws, for example, and seems to be on good terms with them all. But despite these changes in how we think about families, language has not changed to accommodate these new structures at all.

To give an example of the paucity of terminology, my son was trying to make sense of his relationship to my former husband's son by his third marriage. The boys like each other a lot and get on well, even crossing the Atlantic to spend holidays together. They share a sister and two little nephews, but while Luke shares a mother with that sister, Emmet shares a father. So what, they asked, was the best way of describing their relationship. We are not strictly brothers, they reasoned, not even half-brothers; then they came up with a linguistic solution and declared themselves 'quarter-brothers'. I have noticed that occasionally emails go back and forth commencing 'Yo, quarter-bro' which satisfied them both, even though it does sound like the name of a player in some mysterious new sport.

Divorce is, in one respect very sad, but it can also have the effect of extending families, and can bring a great deal of extra interest and companionship into many lives. Perhaps there will be a new vocabulary in time to accommodate the changing world we inhabit, though I am not holding my breath for this to happen in English, given that English is so limited when it comes to family terminology already. Last month, for example, I had some people round for lunch and found myself, as often happens, slightly embarrassed when doing introductions. I could, of course, have simply introduced the six guests to one another by name only, but I have always found it helps to break the ice to give a bit of information, such as 'This is my colleague x', or 'this is one of my oldest friends, y' and so forth. At my lunch, I introduced J. and G. as 'my son-in-law's parents'. The alternative would have been 'my daughter's parents-in-law'. I could have simply said they were friends, which they are, of course, but wanted to signal the family connection. Yet, the English form of describing relations by marriage as 'in-law' has something of a distancing effect, it sounds overly formal and not quite kind. It has often been pointed out that there tend not to be birthday cards on sale with the words 'in-law' attached, and we are all familiar with the notorious mother-in-law jokes of old-style comedians. Yet, J. and G. and I share grandchildren, and there ought to be some way of signalling through language the relationship that we have through our children's marriage. The English in-law phrase seems to hold the family by marriage at arm's length somehow, and that could be because of the origins of the term itself. The first recorded use of in-law dates from the 14th century, from a text of canon law that refers to a 'brother-in-law'. Canon law defined prohibitions, following the incest prohibitions set down in the Old Testament, and we need only think of the excuse used by King Henry VIII to divorce his wife, Catherine of Aragon, to see how seriously such prohibitions were taken. Catherine had been married to Henry's brother, Prince Arthur, and remarriage to a brother-in-law was viewed very negatively. Using the fact that he had married his brother's widow as an excuse, Henry went on to marry five more women with disastrous results all round.

English is not only very limited in its available terminology of relationships by marriage. Other European languages distinguish clearly between maternal and paternal lines; so Danish, for example, has words for grandparents on mother's side – *mormor* and *morfar* and for grandparents on the father's side – *farmor* and *farfar*. Great-grandparents are *oldeforaeldre* (older parents) and my favourite is the alternative for grandparents as *Bedstefar* and *Bedstemor*, with the idea of the specialness of being 'best'. A friend who recently became a grandma told me with delight that the family had opted to call her *Bedstemor*.

Many languages distinguish between cousins and uncles on male and female sides of the family. The Latin word for mother's brother, *avunculus*, has given us the English adjective 'avuncular', with its positive connotations that can be traced back to the high importance of an uncle on the maternal side in early societies. The Latin for father's brother was a different word, *patruus*, while a mother's sister was *amita*.

There is a huge literature on kinship terms, their origins and significance, for the range of terms available to describe the role and position of a family member is directly related to the way in which a particular society is structured. Generalising, there seems to be some similarity in many languages about the existence of terms for immediate family – grandparents, father, mother, son, daughter and so on but beyond that languages vary enormously. Some languages have explicit terms for family members in relation to their age, distinguishing between elder and younger siblings on both father and mother's side of the family. Hungarian seems to have developed a general term for brother and sister only in the 19th century, though it made precise distinctions according to the sibling's place in the family. I am told that Chinese, similarly, has no single term for brother or sister, but a range of terms that locates family members precisely according to their number in the family – seventh son, third youngest uncle and so forth. Translated into English, these terms generally end up as loosely labelled uncle, aunt or cousin, since English does not appear to give much weight to numbers or hierarchy in the same way that traditional Chinese society has done. Some anthropologists have suggested that there are major differences in the classification of kinship systems, with some tending to distinguish predominantly through father and mother systems, others distinguishing more by age. Certainly, the differences in how we use language to talk about our relatives are intriguing.

I found a fascinating account of kinship terminology in Newari, where all kinds of distinctions are made such as 'mother's father's younger brother' and 'grandmother's brother's wife', even, perhaps more relevant in some societies than others, 'mother who has eloped with a paramour' and 'father whose wife has eloped with a paramour'. The implications of that kind of linguistic differentiation in our own society are interesting to reflect upon.

Linked to the question of kinship terms is the way we address our relatives. Many English speakers used, until relatively recently, to use the title of 'uncle 'or 'aunt' as a way of distinguishing special family friends. The problem here is an English problem once again: when you address someone in English, you have to use a name, formally with a title, informally the first name only. For my generation, that convention presented problems to parents who wanted their children to feel a closer connection to their friends than would be signalled by referring to them as Mr or Mrs X, but was more respectful than the child calling an adult by his or her first name.

Other languages have easier ways of greeting one another, and so you can use 'signora' or 'madame' for people you know well or barely know at all, without the slightest discomfort. A friend told me a lovely story about his Italian mother, who had left Italy for Cardiff before the Second World War who used to refer to all her close friends as 'Mrs'- 'Hello Mrs, lovely to see you.' 'Can I get you another cup of tea, Mrs,' a simple transfer of the use of 'signora' made by his mother, who was completely unaware of how strange that sounded in an English-speaking context.

Some African societies have highly complex codes of address, depending on the age, status and kinship of individuals, even down to who is permitted to speak first when encountering someone in the street. Such systems reflect the size of a community, where individuals know who everyone is, and what their place might be. In urban environments that kind of distinction starts to break down, although greeting systems can still be complex in sophisticated cultures, as can be seen in the case of contemporary Japan.

Despite its limitations, perhaps the very poverty of English leads people to greater creativity when it comes to naming family members. I have come across a number of solutions, particularly for the naming of grandparents – Nana and Pompa and GrandDog for a start. Since mine is a divorce-extended family, there are two grandparents on the father's side – Granny and Grandad, and on the mother's side one Great Grandma, then Grandpa and Granny P. in America and one Nonna. My son-in-law very early on added an adjective, and so to the grandsons I am known as Crazy Nonna and addressed as such, which I rather like, since though it may not be the politest form of address, it is funny and unique and perhaps not entirely untrue.

First published in *ITI Bulletin* September–October 2010.

Chapter 38
Rethinking Theory and Practice

One of the tasks that academics often have to take on is to read work submitted for publication to scholarly journals. If you are a member of an editorial board, you will be sent articles for review, and your job is then to write an appraisal that will either give reasons why they should be published, or offer an explanation for rejection. Although all the articles are sent anonymously, so that the reviewer does not know whose work he or she is reading, and the writer does not know who has done the review, I always try to make any criticism potentially helpful by giving suggestions for possible rewriting.

It is important to do this, I believe, since many of the articles are obviously by young people setting out on their academic careers and I remember all too well the sinking feeling I used to have when something I had worked hard at was returned with (in those days) a rejection slip. Sometimes, quite frequently, the work was never returned at all, and so after weeks (or months) of waiting in vain, I would give up and add yet another piece to the increasingly long list of publishing failures. These days, I joke about having once been able to paper a room with rejection slips, but it was less funny at the time.

The other day I had to write a rejection report on an essay that is probably derived from someone's PhD thesis. It is not the first time I have done this of late, and the reason for rejecting most of the pieces I am sent is becoming repetitive: so many of the essays on aspects of translation submitted to journals of literary studies or those devoted to translation reflect an imbalance between the use of translation theory and its practical application.

This latest essay began, as so many of them do, with what is sometimes described as a 'theoretical framework'. The usual suspects were cited, including, unfortunately, myself. There was a quick trot through descriptive translation studies, skopos theory, post-colonialism and the cultural turn. Then the essay started to take off, because finally, after all the regurgitated theories, the author started to get to grips with the translation he or she had been working on, described as 'the case study'. In this, the essay reflects another current trend in scholarly papers and in PhD theses in translation studies: there is a lengthy tracing of different theoretical approaches, followed by something called a case study, which is intended to illustrate the theories. Very occasionally the two are connected, but for the most part, the analysis of the translation is detached from the theory survey. In this latest essay, it was as though the writer had heaved a sigh of relief that the theoretical bit was finally over; the turgid language of the theory section was abandoned, and the translation analysis was well written, lively and showed an understanding of many of the stylistic problems that translators face.

How have we come to this state of affairs? Why do able people, with a clear passion for translation, feel that they have to regurgitate Bassnett or Vermeer or Venuti or Baker or Pym ad infinitum before settling down to analyse texts? It is as though a kind of orthodoxy has come into being, whereby younger scholars feel they cannot get on with the business of translating or studying translations without dutifully reciting a kind of litany of translation theorists. While not wishing to decry some of the valuable insights provided by translation theorists, it does seem as though the pendulum has swung too far in the direction of abstract thinking, with the translations themselves and their translators barely in the picture.

A partial explanation can be found in the emergence of a scholarly field called Translation Studies, and by the desire of some academics to define it as a discipline in its own right. In other words, part of the struggle to create an independent subject area in academia involves trying to find a way of establishing a difference between your field and other fields and then building intellectual fences to create zones in which that field can be promoted. This can involve creating a specialised language, holding specialised seminars, founding specialised journals and so forth, so that specialists can communicate with one another and so acquire more independent status. This is fine in the early days, but there is a real risk that the specialists then end up just talking to themselves.

Thirty years ago, I was one of a small group of scholars who used to meet to argue for the promotion of serious academic study of translation. We were angry young men and women from diverse countries, we challenged orthodoxies and asked awkward questions about why the academic world in general appeared to view translation as low-grade hack work, rather than as a serious and complex process that enables the transfer of meaning across cultures. My background was in comparative literature, a field in which translation, though fundamental and unavoidable when one tries to trace the movement of texts through time and space, was very definitely disparaged. Through my seminars at the University of Warwick on translation and comparative literature, I came to write *Translation Studies*. I intended this book to be a short, easily accessible introduction to the complexities of translation, a simple guide for students wanting to understand more about what translation involves. To my surprise the book did quite well; a second expanded edition followed in 1991, a third in 2002 and editions in other languages continue to appear. Since that book came out, in 1980, there have been dozens of books on translation, demonstrating a huge variety of approaches – books on translation and power, post-colonial translation, translation and interpreting, corpus linguistics and translation, translation and relevance theory, philosophy and translation and many more.

I often read in student essays about how *Translation Studies* was the groundbreaking work that established the discipline. Flattering though that may be, it was never my intention. As I recall, none of us thought we would be creating a new discipline at all; we just wanted to see translations taken more seriously. Nor do I believe, despite the proliferation of books and conferences and dissertations that translation studies really is a discipline, it is simply a means of approaching the ways in which translators work. And despite all the theorising, nothing new is actually being said: Cicero made the basic distinction between literal and free translation 2000 years ago, and all translation theories play around in one way or another with that dichotomy.

Back in 2003, I wrote about translation theory and practice, and asked whether theory could help translators in their day-to-day jobs. At the end of that article, I asked whether the time had come for translation theory to engage more openly with translators. Six years on, I would argue that such engagement is way overdue. When that small group of us used to meet 30 years ago, we were passionate about the need for theory and practice to be interlinked, nourished by and nourishing one another, and we never envisioned a time when theory would sit in one room and practice in another.

Some while ago, I heard the great literary critic Frank Kermode on the radio, talking about how he had changed his mind about the relationship between theory and literary practice. A pioneer of theoretical approaches to literature in the late 1960s and early 1970s, Professor Kermode said he felt the pendulum had swung so far that he was encountering students who only wanted to 'do theory' and could not be bothered with reading writers' actual works. His solution was to go right back to his early lecturing days, and to run theory-less seminars in which students read and discussed actual works by actual writers. The popularity among his students of what appeared now to be a radical approach had convinced him that what some might have viewed as an antediluvian approach was in fact the best way to take literary studies forward. I realised a couple of years ago that I have started to do the same thing.

I am not suggesting that translation theory is useless: if I did, I would be out of a job and would be contradicting decades of research. But I am suggesting that there needs to be more thought given to linking theory with practice, to understanding how translators explain what it is that they do, and how scholars analyse translations. Perhaps one way to ensure closer links is for theorists also to engage in more practice. Interestingly, for several years now students have been voting with their feet to study literature through programmes that offer both critical analysis through reading along with creative writing, and some of the most successful literature degrees have a sizeable writing component.

Recently, a number of literature scholars have started to talk about a 'translational turn' in literary studies, suggesting that translation has increased in importance, that a great many writers are now consciously crossing literary and cultural boundaries in their works, and that literary critics are having to take translation into account in their readings of texts. This development is greatly welcome and long overdue; ironically, it is what those of us who came together 30 years ago were aspiring to. We wanted greater recognition of and understanding of translation, we sought to broaden debates about the role of translation in literary history, about the norms prevailing at different times, about how individual translators went about their task. We were not trying to carve out an independent discipline with its own jargon and boundaries, rather we sought to establish a field of study nourishing and nourished by other disciplines, promoting greater awareness of the movement of texts between languages.

Maybe now, even as I bemoan what seems sometimes to be a widening gap between translation theory and practice, the pendulum is starting to swing back again. I do hope so.

First published in *ITI Bulletin* May–June 2009.

Chapter 39
The Power of Poetry

One of the questions about translation that writers find hardest to answer is: why bother to translate? Of course if a translation is commissioned, then the answer is straightforward, but if someone who only occasionally turns their hand to translating or has perhaps never translated anything before decides to translate, then the question arises as to why he or she has made that particular choice. For, as is widely known, translation is still regarded by some as a sort of inferior relation to 'real' writing, an ugly sister to a Cinderella, and the reasoning behind this attitude is that translation is in some way second class, because the translator is not starting with a blank page but already has someone else's original from which to work.

I have spent a lifetime arguing against this view, protesting that translation is a highly skilled and highly creative activity. Peter Bush (2006: 23) has gone so far as to declare that literary translation is 'the boldest act of writing', and certainly the task of recreating a work written in one language for a completely new set of readers is challenging at best, impossibly difficult at worst. Moreover, if we look at the history of literature, we find a great many writers experimenting with translations; only the other day Tom Paulin's version of *Medea* was in the news, Paulin being yet another in a line of gifted writers who has sought inspiration from the ancient Greeks.

All writing is in some way a rewriting or retelling of other writing, in other words it could be argued that whatever a writer writes is to some extent a kind of translation, because that work will be the product that has emerged out of readings of other people's writing. Sometimes that rewriting will be unconscious, while at other times it will be a deliberate choice. This is particularly the case with poetry, when words and images used by one poet are echoed in the work of another. So, for example, let us take W.H. Auden's famous cry of grief that begins

> Stop all the clocks, cut off the telephone,
> Prevent the dog from barking with a juicy bone,

> Silence the pianos and with muffled drum
> Bring out the coffin, let the mourners come.

This famous poem, which acquired a whole new generation of readers after it was used in the film, *Four Weddings and a Funeral*, is a reworking of a 17th-century poem by Anne Finch, Countess of Winchilsea, which begins:

> Trail all your pikes, dispirit every drum,
> March in a slow procession from afar,
> Be silent, ye dejected Men of war!
> Be still the hautboys and the flute be dumb!

The rhythm of Anne Finch's poem recurs in Auden's, and the image of stilling all joyful or natural sounds in the presence of death is there in both. There are differences, of course: Auden's poem has four verses, Anne Finch's only eight lines, and while his is a poem about the loss of a lover, hers is a poem about the waste of a young life killed for 'your false idol Honour'. Both poems are powerful and moving; Auden expressed his grief through a version that had originated somewhere else, in short, through a form of translation.

I read both the poems years ago, but only recently saw the connection. I have been reading a lot of poetry lately, having suffered the loss of my beloved G. and in the multitude of messages of condolence and support, I have been sent a great many poems in various languages. All, in different ways have been deeply moving and consolatory, and have made me reflect on the vital role played by poetry at times of extreme emotion, whether happiness or grief, for both readers and writers. On the day of G.'s funeral, I received an extraordinary letter from a close friend who is a translator in Sweden, enclosing two poems that she has translated from English, Dilip Chitre's *Ambulance Ride* and David Malouf's version of the five lines written by the Emperor Hadrian, that have proved so difficult for generations of translators because of their succinctness. That poem begins with just three words, 'animula, vagula, blandula' which contain the idea of the smallness and delicacy of a soul released to wander after death. Byron tried his hand at it – 'Ah! gentle, fleeting, wav'ring sprite...' as did so many other poets. Malouf does not even attempt to be succinct, he chooses another strategy altogether and turns the poem into seven stanzas. His translation begins, like the Emperor's, with an address to the wandering soul – 'Dear soul mate, little guest/ and companion' and preserves the idea of the soul being diminutive and afraid as it starts out on its journey to the afterworld. What distinguishes

Malouf's poem is the emphasis he places on the lost playfulness of the soul that is the focus of the final line (nec ut soles dabis jocus), culminating in a powerful final image:

> Without my body
> you're nothing.
> But O, without you, my sweet nothing,
> I'm dust.

Grief, like joy, and the expression of it transcends time and crosses generations. Here translation can play a crucial role, for sometimes the blank page is simply too threatening, its very blankness a reminder of loss. Translating someone else's writing can be a way of easing oneself back into one's own poetry, using the other writer's work as a point of inspiration. Seamus Heaney does this with Dante, while Virgil's account of Aeneas' journey to the Underworld in his *Aeneid* has recurred frequently in various ways in the work of later writers. One writer who has endeavoured to explain this particular creative process is the classical scholar and translator, Josephine Balmer (2006). She relates how she turned to translation when she wanted to write about the death of her beloved niece from cancer:

> But it seemed almost impossible to do this in any direct way. And here I found that a translation could say for me what I could not necessarily say for myself. (Balmer, 2006: 191)

Balmer explains how she found a passage from an epic poem by the fifth-century Roman poet, Claudian, about the abduction of Proserpina by the god of the Underworld, which plunged the world into winter darkness. She recounts how, in order to make her new poem, she translated Claudian faithfully, then added something extra:

> I certainly did not need to tamper with it in any way, except to recontextualize it via a subtitle,' 2/8/:6.47 AM. (Balmer, 2006: 191)

The last lines of her translation, read in the light of that date and time say everything that needs to be said about how she was able to superimpose her own tragedy onto the Roman poet's version of the ancient myth:

> Night scuttled after
> as the light seeped back into our black world
> -everywhere was light

sun and sky and light-
and your small daughter nowhere to be seen. (Balmer, 2006: 191)

By adding the time of the child's death to her translation, Balmer changed the way in which the poem is read. She calls this 'recontextualization', which involves finding a way to rework a translation so that it will serve a new purpose, while at the same time remaining a translation. She cites Michael Longley's similar recontextualisation of a passage from *The Iliad* about the reconciliation between Achilles and King Priam that mirrors the Northern Irish peace process of the early 1990s. Longley is another example of a poet choosing to return to the ancients in order to write about the present, through translation.

Sometime last year, I wrote about trying to give G. a sense of the Spanish poet, Antonio Machado, by trying my hand at translating him, following our visit to Soria where Machado lived. My attempts were not very good, being too literal and shapeless, for I was working too fast and simply trying to provide a 'flavour' of the original. But in the weeks after G.'s death, unable to write anything of my own because the white page was indeed very threatening, I found myself going back to those translations and trying again, not least because the poems I had been working on were those in which Machado writes about the loss of his beloved Leonor, the wife with whom he had shared just three years before she succumbed to tuberculosis.

When I look through the drafts, I can see different writing processes going on: the poems I am making are surely translations, in that I am using Machado's originals as a way of writing about a particular moment in my life that I could not bring myself to write about unaided. Machado's poems transform pain into something beautiful, which serves both as a reminder that human beings have shared the same feelings across time and space throughout history, which is consoling, and as a reminder that poetry, like translation, requires diligence in the use of language.

Central to Machado's writing is a passion for the Castilian landscape that he discovered in adulthood. When I started to translate, I had that landscape in mind, and it was difficult to avoid falling into cliché about tourist-brochure Spain, but now as I recontextualise those poems to become what I would have liked to compose had I been able to do so, the landscape of Castile is becoming Wensleydale, where we lived. The Blue Mountains have become fellsides down which waterfalls erupt after heavy rain, the dusty olive groves have been replaced with the criss-cross patterns of stone walls, the row of poplars beside the river Duero near Soria have become the skeletons of leafless trees along the beck. The landscape of grief in my poems is a northern one, and the lost love is not a young woman as it was for Machado, but an elderly man. So when Machado writes:

> Through these fields of my land
> Bordered by dusty olive groves
> I walk alone,
> Sad, tired, pensive and old. (literal translation)

My version reads:

> Up the track through our field,
> Past the stone laithes, the silent sheep.
> I walk alone
> Tired, sad, full of thoughts and old.

Yet, I would argue that what I am doing is translating, and that if or when I feel these poems are good enough to be read, I will present them as translations. My working title stresses the importance of translation; if this sequence ever sees the light of day, it will be titled 'For Geoffrey. After Machado.'

First published in *ITI Bulletin* March–April 2010.

Select Bibliography

Alvarez, R. and Vidal, A. (eds) (1996) *Translation, Power, Subversion*. Clevedon: Multilingual Matters.
Anderman, G. (2005) *Europe on Stage: Translation and Theatre*. London: Oberon Books.
Anderson, J.J. (ed.) (1996) *Sir Gawain and the Green Knight*. London: Everyman.
Applebaum, S. (trans and ed.) (2007) *Fields of Castile (Campos de Castilla)*. Mineola, NY: Dover Publications.
Apter, E. (2006) *The Translation Zone. A New Comparative Literature*. Princeton: Princeton University Press.
Armitage, S. (2007) *Sir Gawain and the Green Knight*. London: Faber.
Arnold, M. (1857) *On the Modern Element in Literature*. Inaugural Lecture. Oxford: University of Oxford.
Auden, W.H. (1976) *Collected Poems*. London: Faber.
Balmer, J. (2004a) *Chasing Catullus. Poems, Translations and Transgressions*. Tarset: Bloodaxe.
Balmer, J. (2004b) *Catullus. Poems of Love and Hate*. Tarset: Bloodaxe.
Balmer, J. (2006) What comes next? Reconstructing the classics. In S. Bassnett and P. Bush (eds) *The Translator as Writer* (pp. 184–195, 190–191). London: Continuum.
Barnstone, W. (1993) ABC of translating poetry in Barnstone. *The Poetics of Translation. History, Theory, Practice*. New Haven, CT: Yale University Press.
Bassnett, S. (1980) *Translation Studies* (revised 1991; Routledge 2002) Methuen.
Bassnett, S. (2010) *Ted Hughes*. Exeter: Northcote Press.
Bassnett, S. (2005a) Translating terror. *Third World Quarterly* 26, 393–404.
Bassnett, S. (ed.) (2005b) *Global News Translation Special Issue of Language and Intercultural Communication* 5.
Bassnett, S. and Lefevere, A. (eds) (1990) *Translation, History & Culture*. London: Pinter.
Bassnett, S. and Lefevere, A. (1996) *Constructing Cultures: Essays on Literary Translation*. Clevedon: Multilingual Matters.
Bassnett, S. and Trivedi, H. (eds) (1999) *Postcolonial Translation. Theory and Practice*. London: Routledge.
Bassnett, S. with Pizarnik, A. (2002) *Poems and Translations*. Leeds: Peepal Tree.
Bassnett, S. and Bush, P. (eds) (2006) *The Translator as Writer*. London: Continuum.
Benjamin, W. (1992) The task of the translator (H. Zohn, trans.). In R. Schulte and J.Biguenet (eds) *Theories of Translation. An Anthology of Essays from Dryden to Derrida* (pp. 71–82). Chicago: University of Chicago Press.
Beighbeder, F. (2002) *£9.99* (A. Hunter, trans.). London: Picador.

Bhabha, H. (1990) DissemiNation: Time, narrative and the margins of the modern nation. In H. Bhabha (ed.) *Nation and Narration*. London: Routledge.
Bhabha, H. (1994) *The Location of Culture*. London: Routledge.
Bielsa, E. and Bassnett, S. (2009) *Translation in Global News*. London: Routledge.
Borges, J.L. (2002a) In D. Balderston and M.E. Schwartz (trans.) *The Homeric Versions*. In D. Balderston and M.E. Schwartz (eds) *Voice-Overs. Translation and Latin American Literature* (pp. 15–20). Albany, NY: State University of New York Press.
Borges, J.L. (2002b) cited in Efraín Kristal *Invisible Work, Borges and Translation*. Nashville, TN: Vanderbilt University Press.
Brodski, B. (2007) *Can These Bones Live? Translation, Survival and Cultural Memory*. Stanford, CA: Stanford University Press.
Bryce, C. (2005) Six poems. *Modern Poetry in Translation*. Third series, 3.
Burns, P. and Ortiz-Carboneres, S. (trans.) (2002) *Antonio Machado. Lands of Castile and other Poems*. Warminster: Aris and Phillips.
Burton, R. (1880) In I. Burton *Os Lusiadas* (The Lusiads); *Englished by Richard Francis Burton* (2 Vols). London: Bernard Quaritch.
Burton, R. (1881) *Camoens: His Life and His Lusiads. A Commentary by Richard F. Burton* (2 Vols). London: Bernard Quaritch.
Bush, P. and Malmkjaer, K. (eds) (1998) *Rimbaud's Rainbow*. Amsterdam: John Benjamins.
Bush, P. (2006) The writer of translations. In S. Bassnett and P. Bush (eds) *The Translator as Writer* (pp. 23–32). London: Continuum.
Carson, C. (2002) *The Inferno of Dante Alighieri*. London: Granta.
Catford, J.C. (1969) *A Linguistic Theory of Translation: An Essay in Applied Linguistics* London: Oxford University Press.
Chamberlain, L. (1988) Gender and the metaphorics of translation. *Signs* 13, 454–472.
Cheney, D. and Hosington, B.M. (eds and trans.) (2000) *Elizabeth Jane Weston Collected Writings*. Toronto: University of Toronto Press.
Chesterman, A. (1997) *Memes of Translation: The Spread of Ideas in Translation Theory*. Amsterdam: John Benjamins.
Chesterman, A. and Wagner, E. (2002) *Can Theory Help Translators? A Dialogue between the Ivory Tower and the Wordface*. Manchester: St Jerome.
Corbett, J. (1999) *Written in the Language of the Scottish National*. Clevedon: Multilingual Matters.
Cronin, M. (2000) *Across the Lines. Travel, Language, Translation*. Cork: Cork University Press.
Cronin, M. (2006a) *Translation and Globalization*. London: Routledge.
Cronin, M. (2006b) *Translation and Identity*. London: Routledge.
Davidson, P. (ed.) (1999) *The Poems and Translations of Sir Richard Fanshawe* (Vol. 2). Oxford: Clarendon Press.
Davidson, P. (2005) *The Idea of North*. London: Reaktion.
de Campos, A. (1978) *Verso. Reverso, Controverso* (E. Ribeiro Pires Vieira, trans.). San Paolo: Perspectiva.
Diaz Diocaretz, M. (1985) *Translating Poetic Discourse: Questions of Feminist Strategies in Adrienne Rich*. Amsterdam: John Benjamin.
Dingwaney, A. and Meier, C. (eds) (1995) *Between Languages and Cultures: Translation and Cross-Cultural Texts*. Pittsburgh: University of Pittsburgh Press.
Dunn, S. and Scholefield, A. (eds) (1991) *Beneath the Wide Wide Heaven. Poetry of the Environment from Antiquity to the Present*. London: Virago.

Even-Zohar, I. (2000) The position of translated literature within the literary polysystem. In L. Venuti (ed.) *The Translation Studies Reader* (pp. 192–197). London: Routledge.
Eco, U. (2001) *Experiences in Translation*. Toronto: University of Toronto Press.
Eloy Martínez, T. (2002) Trauma and precision in translation. In D. Balderston and M. Schwartz (eds) *Voice-Overs. Translation and Latin American Literature* (pp. 61–63). Albany State, NY: University of New York Press.
Findlay, B. (ed.) (2004) *Frae Ither Tongues. Essays on Modern Translations into Scots*. Clevedon: Multilingual Matters.
Garcia Marquez, G. (2002) The desire to translate. In D. Balderstone and M.E. Schwartz (eds) *Voice-Overs. Translation and Latin-American Literature*. Albany, NY: State University of New York Press.
Gentzler, E. (2001) *Contemporary Translation Theories* (2nd edn). Clevedon: Multilingual Matters.
Gentzler, E. (2006) *Translation and Identity in the Americas*. New York: Routledge.
Godard, B. (1990) Theorizing feminist theory/translation. In S. Bassnett and A. Lefevere (eds) *Translation, History and Culture*. London: Pinter.
Goldsworthy, V. (2009) *Chernobyl Strawberries: A Memoir*. London: Atlantic Books.
Granqvist, R.J. (ed.) (2006) *Writing Back in/and Translation* Frankfurt am Main: Peter Lang.
Hardwick, L. (2000) *Translating Words, Translating Cultures*. London: Duckworth.
Hermans, T. (ed.) (1985) *The Manipulation of Literature*. London: Croom Helm.
Hermans, T. (1999) *Translation in Systems: Descriptive Translation and Systems-Oriented Approaches Explained*. Manchester: St Jerome.
Hermans, T. (2006) *Translating Others*. Manchester: St Jerome.
Hoffman, E. (1989) *Lost in Translation*. London: Heinemann.
Hoffman, E. (2003) PS. In I. de Courtivron (ed.) *Lives in Translation. Bilingual Writers on Identity and Creativity*. London: Palgrave Macmillan.
Holmes, J. (1988) *Translated! Papers on Literary Translation and Translation Studies*. Amsterdam: Rodopi.
Holmes, J. (2000) The name and nature of translation studies. In L. Venuti (ed.) *The Translation Studies Reader* (pp. 172–185). London: Routledge.
Hughes, T. (1999) *The Alcestis of Euripedes*. London: Faber.
Jakobson, R. (2000) On linguistic aspects of translation. In L. Venuti (ed.) *The Translation Studies Reader* (pp. 156–192). London: Routledge.
Kavanagh, P.F. (2000) Ireland's defence-her language. In T. Crowley (ed.) *Language in Ireland 1366–1922/ A Sourcebook* (pp. 204–205). London: Routledge.
Landers, Clifford (2001) *Literary Translation: A Practical Handbook*. Clevedon: Multilingual Matters.
Lefevere, A. (1978) Translation studies: The goal of the discipline. In J.S. Holmes, J. Lambert and R. van den Broeck (eds) *Literature and Translation: New Perspectives in Literary Studies* (pp. 234–235). Leuven: ACCO.
Lefevere, A. (1992a) *Translation, Rewriting and the Manipulation of Literary Fame*. London: Routledge.
Lefevere, A. (ed.) (1992b) *Translation/History/Culture. A Sourcebook*. London: Routledge.
Leppihalme, R. (1997) *Culture Bumps. An Empirical Approach to the Translation of Allusions*. Clevedon: Multilingual Matters.

Levine, S.J. (1991) *The Subversive Scribe: Translating Latin American Fiction*. St Paul: Greywolf Press.
Lianieri, A. and Zajko, V. (eds) (2008) *Translation and the Classic: Identity as Change in the History of Culture*. Oxford: Oxford University Press.
McLynn, Frank (1990) *Burton: Snow Upon the Desert*. London: John Murray.
Morgan, E. (1996) *Collected Translations*. Manchester: Carcanet.
Munday, J. (2001) *Introducing Translation Studies. Theories and Applications*. London: Routledge.
Newbolt, H. (1921) *The Teaching of English in England: Being the Report of the Departmental Committee Appointed by the President of the Board of Education to Enquire into the Position of English in the Educational System*. London: HMSO.
Nida, E. (1964) *Customs and Cultures*. New York: Harper & Row.
Nida, E. (2003) *Towards a Science of Translating: With Special Reference to Principles and Procedures Involved in Bible Translation* (2nd edn). Leiden: Brill.
Niranjana, T. (1992) *Siting Translation: History, Post-Structuralism and the Colonial Context*. Berkeley, CA: University of California Press.
Paz, O. (1992) Translation: literature and letters (I. del Corral, trans.). In R. Schulte and J. Biguenet (eds) *Theories of Translation. An Anthology of Essays from Dryden to Derrida* (pp. 152–162). Chicago: University of Chicago Press.
Pound, E. (1963a) *Cathay*, reprinted in *Ezra Pound: Translations*. New York: New Directions.
Pound, E. (1963b) *Translations*. New York: New Directions.
Pound, E. (1960) *ABC of Reading*. London: Faber and Faber.
Pratt, M.L. (1992) *Imperial Eyes: Travel Writing and Transculturation*. London: Routledge.
Pym, A. (2009) *Exploring Translation Theories*. London: Routledge.
Robinson, D. (1995) Theorising translation in a woman's voice: Subverting the rhetoric of patronage, courtly love and morality. *The Translator* 1, 153–175.
Rossant, C. (2004) *Apricots on the Nile*. New York: Atria.
Rossant, C. (2003) *Return to Paris*. New York: Atria.
Sapir, E. (1956) *Culture, Language and Personality*. Berkeley, CA: University of California Press.
Schaeffner, C. and Bassnett, S. (eds) (2010) *Political Discourse, Media and Translation*. Newcastle upon Tyne: Cambridge Scholars Publishing.
Simon, S. (1996) *Gender in Translation. Cultural Identity and the Politics of Transmission*. London: Routledge.
Simon, S. (2006) *Translating Montreal. Episodes in the Life of a Divided City*. Montreal and Kingston: McGill-Queen's University Press.
Snell-Hornby, M. (2006) *The Turns of Translation Studies. New Paradigms or Shifting Viewpoints?* Amsterdam: John Benjamins.
Steiner, G. (1998) *After Babel: Aspects of Language and Translation* (2nd edn). Oxford: Oxford University Press.
Tomlinson, C. (1982) *Poetry and Metamorphosis*. Cambridge: Cambridge University Press.
Toury, G. (1995) *Descriptive Translation Studies and Beyond*. Amsterdam: John Benjamins.

Toury, G. (1999) A handful of paragraphs on 'translation' and 'norms' In C. Schaeffner (ed.) *Translation and Norms* (pp. 9–31). Clevedon: Multilingual Matters.
Tsai, C. (2005) Inside the television newsroom: An insider's view of international news translation in Taiwan. *Language and Intercultural Communication* 5, Special issue *Global News Translation* S. Bassnett (ed.) (pp. 145–153).
Tymoczko, M. (2009) Translation, ethics and ideology in a violent globalizing world. In E. Bielsa and C.W. Hughes (eds) *Globalization, Political Violence and Translation* (pp. 171–194). London: Palgrave.
Tymoczko, M. and Gentzler, E. (eds) (2002) *Translation and Power*. Amherst and Boston: University of Massachusetts Press.
Vanderplank, R. (2007) *Uglier Than a Monkey's Armpit. Untranslateable Insults, Put-Downs and Curses from around the World*. London: Boxtree.
Venuti, L. (ed.) (1992) *Rethinking Translation*. London: Routledge.
Venuti, L. (1995) *The Translator's Invisibility: A History of Translation*. London: Routledge.
Venuti, L. (1998) *The Scandals of Translation. Towards an Ethics of Difference* London: Routledge.
Venuti, L. (ed.) (2000) *The Translation Studies Reader*. London: Routledge.
Vermeer, H. J. (2000) Skopos and commission in translational action (A. Chesterman, trans.). In L. Venuti (ed.) *The Translation Studies Reader* (pp. 221–232). London: Routledge.
Vieira, Else Ribeiro Pires (1999) Liberating Calibans: Readings of Antropofagia and Haroldo de Campos' poetics of transcreation. In S. Bassnett and H. Trivedi (eds) *Postcolonial Translation: Theory and Practice* (pp. 95–113). London: Routledge.
Weinberger, E. (2002) *Anonymous Sources: A Talk on Translators and Translation*. In D. Balderston and M. Schwartz (eds) *Voice-Overs. Translation and Latin American Literature* (pp. 104–118). Albany, NY: State University of New York Press.
Weinberger, E. and Paz, O. (eds) (1987) *Nineteen Ways of Looking at Wang Wei*. Mt Kisco, NY: Moyer Bell.
Young, R. (2006) Writing back, in Translation. In R.J. Grandqvist (ed.) *Writing Back in/and Translation* (pp. 19–38). Frankfurt: Peter Lang.

For Product Safety Concerns and Information please contact our EU Authorised Representative:

Easy Access System Europe

Mustamäe tee 50

10621 Tallinn

Estonia

gpsr.requests@easproject.com

www.ingramcontent.com/pod-product-compliance
Ingram Content Group UK Ltd.
Pitfield, Milton Keynes, MK11 3LW, UK
UKHW021941200326
4879IPUK00004B/43